THE ECOMMERCE PLAYBOOK

Strategies for Building a Thriving Online Business

ROBIN O'LIST

TABLE OF CONTENTS

INTRODUCTION

Are you ready to take your eCommerce business to the next level? Look no further than *The eCommerce Playbook*. In this book, you'll find all the tools, tips, and strategies you need to create a successful online store.

I have been working in the eCommerce industry since 2010 and over the years I have tried and tested numerous strategies. My goal is to share my strategies with you so that you can build your eCommerce business faster.

In today's digital age, eCommerce has become an increasingly popular way for entrepreneurs to start and grow their businesses. With the rise of online shopping and the convenience it offers, eCommerce businesses have the potential to reach a global audience and generate significant revenue.

However, building an eCommerce business is not as simple as setting up a website and waiting for customers to come. There are many aspects to consider, from choosing the right platform and designing a user-friendly website, to sourcing products, managing inventory, and marketing effectively. It can be overwhelming to navigate these various components, especially if you're new to the world of eCommerce.

That's why I have created this comprehensive guide to help you build a successful eCommerce business from the ground up. Whether you're starting from scratch or looking to improve an existing business, this guide will provide you with the knowledge and tools you need to create a profitable and sustainable eCommerce enterprise. So, let's get started

THE BUSINESS PLAN

Starting with a solid business plan is essential for setting goals, and identifying your target market, products, and pricing strategy when starting an eCommerce business.

A business plan is a roadmap that outlines your business goals, target market, products, marketing strategies, and financial projections. It provides a clear framework for how you will achieve your goals and what steps you need to take to build a successful eCommerce business.

One of the first steps in creating a business plan is setting goals and objectives. This includes identifying your long-term and short-term goals, such as revenue targets, growth targets, and customer acquisition goals. It is important to make sure your goals are Specific, Measurable, Achievable, Relevant, and Time-bound (SMART).

Once you have established your goals, you can begin to identify your target market. This involves creating a customer persona and identifying the demographics and psychographics of your ideal customer. You can also analyze the market and competition to understand the demand for your products and services and identify gaps in the market that you can fill.

Next, you will need to identify the products you will offer and your pricing strategy. This involves identifying the features and benefits of your products, determining your cost of goods sold, and setting your prices to ensure profitability while remaining competitive in the market. It's important to consider factors such as shipping costs, taxes, and payment processing fees when setting your prices.

Finally, your business plan should outline your marketing and sales strategies. This includes identifying the channels you will use to reach your target audiences, such as social media, email marketing, or paid advertising. You should also consider how you will measure the success of your marketing efforts and adjust your strategies as needed.

Here are the key elements you should include when writing a business plan for an eCommerce business:

1. **Executive summary:** This section should provide an overview of your business, including your mission statement, products or services, target market, and financial goals.

2. **Market analysis:** Conduct research on your industry and target market. Include information on market size, growth trends, customer needs, and the competitive landscape.

3. **Products and services:** Describe the products or services you plan to offer, including their features, benefits, and pricing strategy.

4. **Marketing and sales strategy:** Explain how you plan to promote your eCommerce business and attract customers. This can include tactics such as social media advertising, email marketing, influencer partnerships, and SEO.

5. **Operations plan:** Detail how your eCommerce business will operate, including order fulfillment, inventory management, shipping and handling, and customer service.

6. **Financial projections:** Provide detailed financial projections for your eCommerce business, including startup costs, revenue projections, and expenses. This should also include a break-even analysis and cash flow projections.

7. **Management team:** Highlight the key members of your management team and their relevant experience in eCommerce, retail, marketing, or finance.

8. **Risk analysis:** Identify potential risks to your eCommerce business, such as changes in the competitive landscape, shifts in consumer behavior, or supply chain disruptions.

Overall, starting with a solid business plan can help you set goals, identify your target market, products, and pricing strategy, and create a roadmap for building a successful eCommerce business. It provides a clear framework for how you will achieve your goals and helps ensure that you stay focused and on track.

CHOOSING THE RIGHT PRODUCT

Choosing a niche or product that you're passionate about and has high demand in the market is essential for building a successful eCommerce business.

Firstly, choosing a niche or product you're passionate about can help you stay motivated and engaged in your business. When you're passionate about what you're selling, it becomes easier to put in the time and effort required to build a successful eCommerce business. You're also more likely to have a deep understanding of your niche or product, which can help you create high-quality content and provide excellent customer service.

Secondly, choosing a niche or product with high demand in the market can help ensure that there is a customer base for your products. This means that there is an existing demand for the products you're selling, which can make it easier to attract and retain customers. It can also help you stay competitive in the market and make it easier to generate revenue and profits.

When choosing a niche or product, it's important to conduct thorough market research to identify gaps in the market and understand the needs and preferences of your target audience. You should also analyze your competition and identify its strengths and weaknesses to ensure you can differentiate yourself and offer unique value to your customers.

Following these steps will help you select the best niche or product for your eCommerce business:

1. **Conduct market research:** Conduct research on different markets and industries to identify trends and opportunities. Use online tools such as Google Trends, Amazon Best Sellers, and social media to help you gather information.

2. **Evaluate market demand:** Evaluate market demand for your potential products by analyzing search volume, consumer interest, and competitor analysis. You can use tools such as Google Keyword Planner, SEMrush, and Ahrefs to help you with this analysis.

3. **Identify your target audience:** Identify the specific audience you want to target. Consider factors such as age, gender, income, and interests to help you identify the best niche or product for your target audience.

4. **Check product viability:** Check the viability of your product by assessing its manufacturing costs, shipping costs, and profit margins. You should also consider whether your product is easy to source and whether there is demand for it in your target market.

5. **Consider your passion and expertise:** Consider your own interests and expertise when selecting a niche or product. Choose a niche or product that you are passionate about and have knowledge of, as this can help you stay motivated and build a stronger brand identity.

6. **Evaluate competition:** Evaluate the competition in your potential niche or product category. Check how many competitors you have, their prices, and their marketing strategies. Consider whether you can differentiate your product or service and offer better value to your target audience.

7. **Evaluate your idea:** Before committing fully to a niche or product, consider evaluating your idea with a small-scale launch or trial. This can help you identify any issues or challenges before investing considerable time and resources into your eCommerce business.

In conclusion, selecting the right niche or product for your eCommerce business requires careful consideration of market demand, target audience, product viability, competition, and your own passion and expertise. By taking these steps, you can increase the likelihood of success and build a profitable eCommerce business.

MARKET RESEARCH

Conducting thorough market research is essential for identifying your target audience, their needs, and preferences when starting an eCommerce business.

Market research involves gathering and analyzing information about your industry, competitors, and target audience. This can include analyzing trends and market conditions, identifying gaps in the market, and understanding the buying behavior and preferences of your target audience.

One of the first steps in conducting market research is identifying your target audience. This involves creating a customer persona, which is a detailed description of your ideal customer. This can include demographic information such as age, gender, location, and income, as well as psychographic information such as interests, values, and behavior.

Once you have identified your target audience, you can conduct research to understand their needs and preferences. This can include analyzing social media conversations, conducting surveys, and gathering feedback from customer reviews. You can also consider analyzing data from competitor websites and online marketplaces to understand the products and services that are in demand.

In addition to understanding your target audience, it's also important to analyze your competition. This can include identifying your direct and indirect competitors, analyzing their strengths and weaknesses, and understanding their pricing and marketing strategies.

Here are some steps you can take to conduct market research and identify your target audience:

1. **Define your product or service:** Start by defining your product or service, including its features, benefits, and unique selling points. This will help you understand what your business offers and how it can meet the needs of your target audience.

2. **Identify your competitors:** Identify your competitors and analyze their products or services, pricing, and marketing strategies. This will help you understand the current market landscape and identify gaps or opportunities in the market.

3. **Conduct surveys and interviews:** Conduct surveys and interviews with potential customers to gather information on their needs, preferences, and behaviors. You can use online survey tools such as SurveyMonkey or Google Forms to conduct surveys, and you can reach out to potential customers through social media, email, or other channels.

4. **Analyze demographic data:** Analyze demographic data such as age, gender, income, and location to help you identify your target audience. You can use online tools such as the US Census Bureau or Statista to gather demographic data.

5. **Use social media analytics:** Use social media analytics to gather information on your potential customers. You can use tools such as Facebook Insights, Twitter Analytics, or Instagram Insights to gather information on your audience's interests, behaviors, and demographics.

6. **Analyze website and search engine data:** Analyze website and search engine data to understand how potential customers are finding and interacting with your website. You can use tools such as Google Analytics to gather information on website traffic, bounce rates, and search engine rankings.

7. **Develop buyer personas:** Based on the information you have gathered, develop buyer personas that represent your target audience. These personas should include information on demographics, needs, behaviors, and pain points, and will help you better understand and connect with your target audience.

In conclusion, conducting thorough market research is critical to identifying your target audience for your eCommerce business. By defining your product or service, analyzing competitors, conducting surveys and interviews, analyzing demographic and social media data, analyzing website and search engine data, and developing buyer personas, you can gain valuable insights into your target audience and build a stronger, more successful eCommerce business.

USER-FRIENDLY WEBSITE

First off, let's talk about what we mean by "user-friendly." A user-friendly website is easy to navigate, visually appealing, and provides a positive user experience. It's a website that's designed with your audience in mind and makes it easy for them to find what they're looking for.

Now, why is this so important? Well, for starters, a user-friendly website can increase your website traffic and engagement. If your website is easy to use, visitors are more likely to stick around and explore what you have to offer. This can lead to more page views, longer visit times, and ultimately, more conversions.

But that's not all. A user-friendly website can also improve your brand reputation and credibility. If visitors have a positive experience on your website, they're more likely to trust your brand and recommend it to others.

On the other hand, a poorly designed and difficult-to-use website can have the opposite effect. Visitors may become frustrated and leave your website, resulting in a high bounce rate and low engagement. This can damage your brand's reputation and lead to a loss of potential customers.

So, there you have it - creating a user-friendly website is crucial for your online success. By providing a positive user experience, you can increase website traffic, improve brand reputation, and ultimately, drive more conversions.

1. **User-friendly design:** A user-friendly design is essential for keeping visitors on your site and encouraging them to explore your content. To achieve this, your website should have a clear and intuitive navigation structure that makes it easy for visitors to find what they are looking for. Additionally, the website's layout should be visually appealing, with a consistent color scheme and font style that enhances the user experience.

2. **Mobile responsiveness:** With more than 50% of website traffic coming from mobile devices, it's critical to ensure your website is mobile-responsive. This means that your website's design and layout should adapt to different screen sizes to provide a seamless browsing experience for visitors using smartphones and tablets.

3. **Search engine optimization (SEO):** SEO involves optimizing your website's content and structure to rank higher in search engine results pages (SERPs). This requires incorporating relevant keywords into your content, optimizing your website's metadata, and ensuring that your website's structure is search-engine friendly.

4. **Content quality:** Your website's content is the foundation of its user experience and SEO. High-quality content that provides value to your audience can help to increase engagement and conversions. When creating content, it's important to consider the user's intent and provide relevant information that meets their needs.

5. **Site speed:** Site speed is a critical factor in user experience and SEO. A slow-loading website can result in a high bounce rate, which negatively impacts your SEO ranking. To optimize site speed, minimize the size of images and videos, reduce the number of HTTP requests, and enable browser caching.

In summary, creating a user-friendly and visually appealing website that is optimized for search engines requires a combination of design, functionality, and content. By prioritizing the user experience and implementing effective SEO strategies, you can attract and retain visitors while also increasing your website's visibility in search results.

MOBILE-FRIENDLY WEBSITE

A mobile-friendly website design is like a superhero cape for your website! It's optimized to give users a seamless browsing experience, no matter what mobile device they're using. This kind of web design is crafted with responsive design techniques, which enables your website to adapt to the screen size and resolution of the device. So, whether your user is browsing on an iPhone or an Android tablet, your site looks just as amazing and intuitive.

But wait, there's more! A mobile-friendly website design takes into account the limitations of mobile devices such as slow loading times and limited bandwidth. It aims to provide a streamlined user experience that is easy to navigate with clear and concise content and blazing-fast load times. This means that your users are not only getting a visually stunning experience but also a practical one that is effortless and frustration-free.

The goal of any website design is to ensure that visitors to your site have an amazing user experience, no matter what device they're using. So, if you want to attract more users to your website, keep them engaged, and make them want to come back, you need a mobile-friendly design that makes your website shine like a superhero!

If your website isn't optimized for mobile, you risk alienating a sizable chunk of your audience with slow loading times, awkward navigation, and an overall terrible user experience. And let's be honest, nobody wants that!

But it's not just about pleasing your users. Search engines like Google prioritize mobile-friendly websites in their search results, meaning your site may not even show up on the first page if it's not mobile optimized. So, you're not just risking a bad user experience; you're also missing out on valuable traffic and potential customers.

That's why it's essential for businesses and organizations to ensure their website is mobile optimized. Don't let your website fall behind the times and lose out on engagement and customers. Get ahead of the game and give your users the seamless experience they deserve, no matter what device they're using.

1. **Improved user experience:** A mobile-friendly website provides a better user experience for visitors using mobile devices. A responsive design ensures that your website's content is easy to read and navigate on smaller screens, reducing the need for users to zoom in or out or scroll horizontally to view content.

2. **Increased engagement:** A mobile-friendly website can lead to increased engagement rates, as visitors are more likely to stay on your website for longer periods of time. A website that is easy to use and navigate on mobile devices can encourage visitors to explore your content and take action.

3. **Higher search engine rankings:** In 2015, Google announced that it would be using mobile friendliness as a ranking factor in search results. Websites that are not optimized for mobile devices are likely to rank lower in search engine results pages, leading to reduced visibility and traffic.

4. **Greater accessibility:** A mobile-friendly website is more accessible to a wider audience, including those with disabilities. A responsive design ensures that users with visual or motor impairments can easily navigate and interact with your website on their mobile devices.

5. **Competitive advantage:** With more businesses realizing the importance of mobile optimization, having a mobile-friendly website can give you a competitive advantage. A website that is easy to use and navigate on mobile devices can help to build trust and credibility with your audience, leading to increased conversions and customer loyalty.

To ensure your website is mobile-friendly and responsive to different devices and screen sizes, there are a few key steps you can take:

1. **Use a responsive design:** A responsive design ensures that your website's layout and content adapt to different screen sizes and resolutions. This includes using flexible grids, responsive images and videos, and touch-friendly navigation.

2. **Optimize for mobile speed:** Mobile users are often on-the-go and have less time to wait for a website to load. To optimize for mobile speed, minimize the size of images and videos, reduce the number of HTTP requests, and enable browser caching.

3. **Test your website on different devices:** To ensure that your website is optimized for different devices and screen sizes, it's important to test it on a variety of smartphones and tablets. This can help you identify any issues with layout, functionality, or performance.

4. **Prioritize mobile-friendly content:** When creating content for your website, prioritize mobile-friendly formats such as short paragraphs, bullet points, and concise headlines. Avoid using large blocks of text or complicated formatting that can be difficult to read on smaller screens.

In conclusion, ensuring your website is mobile-friendly and responsive to different devices and screen sizes is essential for providing a positive user experience, increasing engagement rates, and improving your search engine rankings. By using a responsive design, optimizing for the mobile speed, testing on different devices, and prioritizing mobile-friendly content, you can create a website that meets the needs of your mobile audience and helps to grow your business.

SECURE AND RELIABLE ECOMMERCE PLATFORM

An eCommerce platform is a software application that allows businesses to build and manage their online store. When choosing an eCommerce platform, it's important to consider security and reliability. Here are some factors to look for when choosing a secure and reliable eCommerce platform:

1. **PCI compliance:** The Payment Card Industry Data Security Standard (PCI DSS) is a set of security standards designed to protect credit card information during transactions. Look for an eCommerce platform that is PCI compliant to ensure that your customer's payment information is protected.

2. **SSL encryption:** Secure Sockets Layer (SSL) is a security protocol that encrypts data between a website and a user's web browser. Look for an eCommerce platform that uses SSL encryption to ensure that sensitive information, such as login credentials and payment information, is protected from hackers.

3. **Regular security updates:** A good eCommerce platform should regularly update its software to patch security vulnerabilities and improve the overall security of the platform. Make sure that the platform you choose provides regular security updates and patches.

4. **Fraud detection and prevention:** Look for an eCommerce platform that offers fraud detection and prevention features. These features can help to protect your business from chargebacks and other types of fraud.

5. **Secure hosting:** The hosting environment can have a significant impact on the security and reliability of an eCommerce platform. Look for a platform that uses secure and reliable hosting providers that offer features such as 24/7 monitoring and backups.

6. **Multi-factor authentication:** Multi-factor authentication adds an extra layer of security to the login process by requiring users to provide additional information, such as a code sent to their phone or email. Look for an eCommerce platform that offers multi-factor authentication to prevent unauthorized access to your store.

7. **Reputation and reviews:** Do some research on the reputation and reviews of the eCommerce platform you are considering. Look for reviews from other businesses that have used the platform to get an idea of the platform's security and reliability.

8. **Customer support:** Look for an eCommerce platform that provides good customer support. In the event of a security breach or other issue, you want to be able to get support from the platform provider quickly and easily.

In conclusion, choosing a secure and reliable eCommerce platform is crucial for the success of your online business. Look for a platform that is PCI compliant, uses SSL encryption, provides regular security updates, offers fraud detection and prevention features, uses secure hosting, offers multi-factor authentication, has a good reputation and reviews, and provides good customer support. By choosing a secure and reliable platform, you can protect your business and your customers and ensure the smooth operation of your online store.

Here are the top five eCommerce platforms.

There are numerous eCommerce platforms available in the market, but here are the top five eCommerce platforms and their features that make them stand out:

1. **Shopify:** Shopify is one of the most popular eCommerce platforms in the world, with over 1 million businesses using it to sell their products online. It is known for its ease of use, customizable themes, and strong support for multiple payment options. Shopify also offers a range of add-ons and plugins, including social media integration, abandoned cart recovery, and email marketing tools.

2. **WooCommerce:** WooCommerce is an eCommerce plugin for WordPress, one of the most widely used website builders in the world. WooCommerce is free and open source, and it offers a range of customization options, including themes and plugins. It is known for its ease of use and flexibility, making it a popular choice for small businesses and startups.

3. **BigCommerce:** BigCommerce is a cloud-based eCommerce platform that is known for its scalability and enterprise-level features. It offers a range of features, including customizable themes, advanced SEO tools, and multi-channel selling options. BigCommerce is popular among businesses that want to scale quickly and need an eCommerce platform that can handle high traffic and large product catalogs.

4. **Magento:** Magento is an open-source eCommerce platform that is known for its flexibility and customization options. It is popular among medium to large-sized businesses that need a highly customizable platform. Magento offers a range of features, including advanced product management, marketing tools, and multi-language support.

5. **Squarespace:** Squarespace is a website builder that also offers eCommerce functionality. It is known for its modern and visually appealing templates and an easy-to-use drag-and-drop interface. Squarespace also offers features such

as abandoned cart recovery, inventory management, and multi-channel selling options.

Overall, the top eCommerce platforms offer a range of features and customization options to suit different business needs. Shopify and WooCommerce are popular among small businesses and startups, while BigCommerce and Magento are more geared toward medium to large-sized businesses. Squarespace is a good option for businesses that want a simple and visually appealing eCommerce platform. Ultimately, the choice of an eCommerce platform will depend on your business needs, budget, and technical expertise.

SHIPPING AND RETURN POLICIES

When it comes to shopping online, the experience can be a bit like a blind date. You never quite know what you're going to get until it arrives at your doorstep. That's why having clear and prominent shipping and return policies on your eCommerce website is a must-have!

First of all, shipping and return policies give your customers a clear understanding of what to expect when they make a purchase. Nobody wants to be surprised by unexpected shipping fees or find out that they can't return an item after they've already bought it.

Plus, by displaying your policies prominently on your website, you're showing your customers that you're transparent and trustworthy. This builds trust and confidence in your brand and can help turn one-time buyers into loyal customers.

But wait, there's more! Having clear shipping and return policies can also save you time and money. By providing your customers with clear instructions on how to return items or what to do if they haven't received their order, you can reduce the number of customer service inquiries and disputes.

Shipping Policy:

Your shipping policy should clearly outline the following information:

1. **Shipping rates:** Specify your shipping rates, whether it be a flat rate or based on the order's weight or destination.

2. **Shipping options:** Mention the different shipping options available, such as standard, expedited, or overnight shipping.

3. **Delivery times:** Be sure to include estimated delivery times for each shipping option to set clear expectations.

4. **Order processing time:** Specify the time required to process orders before shipping them.

5. **Shipping carrier:** Provide details about the shipping carriers you use.

6. **Shipping restrictions:** Specify any items that cannot be shipped or any restrictions on shipping to certain locations.

Return Policy:

Your return policy should be clear and easy to understand to avoid confusion or frustration for customers. Here are some key aspects to include in your return policy:

1. **Return window:** Clearly define the time window within which customers can return items, such as 30 days after delivery.

2. **Return process:** Provide instructions on how customers can initiate a return and what information they need to provide.

3. **Return condition:** State the condition in which the product should be returned, such as unused, unopened, or in its original packaging.

4. **Refund process:** Explain how refunds will be processed, such as whether they will be issued to the original payment method or as store credit.

5. **Return shipping:** Clearly specify who is responsible for the return shipping cost, whether it be the customer or the business.

The importance of shipping and return policies:

1. **Building trust:** Having clear and transparent shipping and return policies can build trust with customers, helping to establish your business as dependable and customer focused.

2. **Reducing customer confusion:** A well-defined shipping and return policy can reduce customer confusion and frustration, helping to improve the overall customer experience.

3. **Setting expectations:** Clearly outlining shipping rates, delivery timeframes, and return windows can set clear expectations for customers and reduce the likelihood of misunderstandings or disputes.

4. **Increasing conversions:** A clear and easy-to-understand shipping and return policy can increase customer confidence, leading to a higher likelihood of completing a purchase.

5. **Improving reputation:** Providing a positive customer experience through your shipping and return policies can lead to positive reviews and recommendations, helping to improve your business's reputation.

In short, having clear and prominent shipping and return policies on your eCommerce website is essential for building trust, reducing disputes, and keeping your customers happy. So, don't be afraid to flaunt those policies like a peacock and let your customers know that you've got their back!

HASSLE-FREE RETURNS AND EXCHANGES

Picture this: You've just ordered a new pair of shoes online, and when they arrive, they don't fit quite right. But, when you try to return or exchange them, the process is so complicated that you end up keeping the shoes and feeling frustrated with the company. Don't be that company!

Offering hassle-free returns and exchanges on your eCommerce website is a game-changer! Not only does it make your customers feel more confident in making a purchase, but it also shows that you care about their satisfaction.

With easy returns and exchanges, your customers can feel comfortable taking a chance on your products without the fear of getting stuck with something that doesn't work for them. This means more sales and more satisfied customers who are likely to return to your website time and time again.

But the benefits don't stop there! Offering hassle-free returns and exchanges can also help reduce the number of customer service inquiries and complaints. It's a win-win situation for both you and your customers.

1. **Increases customer satisfaction:** Customers appreciate the option to return or exchange products that don't meet their expectations. By offering an easy and hassle-free return process, eCommerce brands can increase customer satisfaction and build loyalty.

2. **Builds trust:** By offering a transparent and straightforward return policy, eCommerce brands can build trust with their customers. This can help to establish the brand as reliable and customer-focused, which can encourage repeat purchases and positive word-of-mouth referrals.

3. **Reduces cart abandonment:** Customers are more likely to make a purchase if they know they can easily return or exchange the product if they're not satisfied. By offering an easy return process, eCommerce brands can reduce cart abandonment and encourage customers to complete their purchases.

4. **Improves brand reputation:** By offering an easy and hassle-free return process, eCommerce brands can improve their reputation in the industry. This can help to attract new customers and establish the brand as a leader in the eCommerce space.

5. **Increases sales:** Offering an easy return process can increase customer confidence and encourage more people to make a purchase. This can lead to increased sales and revenue for the eCommerce brand.

So, don't be afraid to make returns and exchanges easy as pie! It's a small investment that can pay off big time in customer satisfaction, repeat business, and your bottom line. Let your customers know that you've got their backs, and they'll reward you with their loyalty.

PAYMENT OPTIONS

When running an eCommerce business, offering multiple payment options is essential for providing a seamless and convenient checkout experience for customers. Here are some reasons why offering multiple payment options is important, along with some tips for implementing them effectively:

1. **Convenience for customers:** By offering multiple payment options, you provide customers with the flexibility to choose the payment method that is most convenient and comfortable for them. This can help to reduce cart abandonment rates and increase conversion rates, as customers are more likely to complete their purchases if they have the option to pay using their preferred payment method.

2. **Global reach:** Offering multiple payment options can also help you to expand your customer base and reach a global audience. Different countries and regions have different preferred payment methods, so by offering a variety of options, you can cater to the

preferences of customers in different locations and increase your reach.

3. **Reduced risk of fraud:** By offering multiple payment options, you can reduce the risk of fraud and chargebacks. Different payment methods have different levels of security and fraud protection, so by offering multiple options, you give customers the ability to choose the payment method that they feel most secure using.

Tips for implementing multiple payment options:

1. **Offer popular payment methods:** Start by offering the most popular payment methods, such as credit/debit cards, PayPal, and Apple Pay. These are widely accepted and trusted by customers, making them a safe bet for most eCommerce businesses.

2. **Consider regional preferences:** Depending on your target audience and location, there may be other payment methods that are more popular or preferred. For example, in some regions, cash on delivery or bank transfers may be the preferred payment method. Be sure to research the payment preferences of your target audience and offer options that cater to their needs.

3. **Display payment options prominently:** Make sure that customers can easily see the payment options that you offer. Display them prominently on your website, especially on the

checkout page, to make it clear and easy for customers to choose the payment method that they prefer.

4. **Ensure security:** Ensure that all payment options that you offer are secure and reliable. Use trusted payment gateways and ensure that your website is secured with SSL to protect customer information.

5. **Simplify the checkout process:** Make the checkout process as simple and streamlined as possible. Offer an express checkout option for returning customers and make it easy for customers to save their payment information for future purchases.

6. **Test and optimize:** Test different payment options and monitor their performance. Use analytics tools to track conversion rates and identify any issues or drop-offs in the checkout process. Continuously optimize and improve the checkout process based on customer feedback and data analysis.

In conclusion, offering multiple payment options is essential for eCommerce businesses that want to provide a seamless and convenient checkout experience for customers. By offering popular payment methods, considering regional preferences, displaying payment options prominently, ensuring security, simplifying the checkout process, and testing and optimizing regularly, you can create an effective and customer-friendly payment experience that helps to increase conversion rates and grow your business.

FAST AND AFFORDABLE SHIPPING

Offering fast and affordable shipping options with tracking is an important aspect of any eCommerce business. Customers expect timely and reliable delivery of their orders and providing them with multiple shipping options and the ability to track their orders can help to build trust and loyalty.

You might not be able to compete with the likes of Amazon with next day delivery, but you should be aiming for the fastest and most affordable delivery options you can find.

Here are five ways you can offer fast and affordable shipping options with tracking:

1. **Choose a dependable shipping partner:** Partnering with a dependable shipping carrier is crucial for ensuring fast and efficient delivery. Research different shipping carriers and choose one that has a good reputation for on-time delivery and tracking accuracy.

2. **Offer multiple shipping options:** Offering customers multiple shipping options can provide them with flexibility and help to ensure

that they receive their orders in a timely manner. Consider offering options like standard, expedited, and overnight shipping, and provide estimated delivery times for each option.

3. **Set clear shipping rates:** Providing transparent and clear shipping rates can help to avoid confusion and frustration for customers. Consider offering flat-rate shipping or free shipping for orders above a certain value.

4. **Provide order tracking:** Providing customers with the ability to track their orders can help to build trust and confidence in your eCommerce business. Offer tracking information via email or through a customer account page on your website.

5. **Use packaging materials that protect the product:** Protecting the products during shipping can help to ensure that they arrive in good condition. Consider using packaging materials like bubble wrap, packing peanuts, or air pillows to provide cushioning and protection.

Here are four benefits of offering fast and affordable shipping options with tracking:

1. **Increased customer satisfaction:** Offering fast and affordable shipping options with tracking can improve customer satisfaction and loyalty. Customers are more likely to return to your website and recommend your business to others if they have a positive shipping experience.

2. **Reduced cart abandonment:** High shipping costs or slow delivery times are common reasons for cart abandonment. Offering affordable and fast shipping options can reduce cart abandonment rates and increase conversions.

3. **Competitive advantage:** Offering fast and affordable shipping options with tracking can give your eCommerce business a competitive advantage over others. Customers are more likely to choose your business over competitors if you offer better shipping options and rates.

4. **Improved reputation:** Providing customers with a positive shipping experience can help to improve your business's reputation and credibility. Positive reviews and recommendations from satisfied customers can help to attract new customers and grow your business.

In summary, offering fast and affordable shipping options with tracking is an important aspect of eCommerce business. Choose a dependable shipping partner, offer multiple shipping options, set clear shipping rates, provide order tracking, and use packaging materials that protect the product. By doing so, you can improve customer satisfaction, reduce cart abandonment, gain a competitive advantage, and improve your business's reputation.

FREE SHIPPING OPTIONS

Offering free shipping for customers who spend a certain amount on eCommerce stores can have multiple benefits for both the customers and the business, including:

1. **Increased sales:** Customers are more likely to make a purchase if they know that they can get free shipping by spending a certain amount. This can help increase sales and encourage customers to purchase more items.

2. **Higher order value:** By setting a minimum order value for free shipping, businesses can encourage customers to spend more money on a single transaction. This can help increase the average order value and ultimately increase revenue.

3. **Improved customer loyalty:** Offering free shipping can improve customer loyalty by providing an added incentive for customers to shop with your business. Customers are more likely to return to a store where they have had a positive shopping experience.

4. **Competitive advantage:** Offering free shipping can also give businesses a competitive advantage over their competitors. In a crowded marketplace, free shipping can be the deciding factor for customers when choosing between two similar businesses.

5. **Reduced cart abandonment:** High shipping costs are a common reason for cart abandonment. By offering free shipping for a certain minimum order value, businesses can reduce the likelihood of customers abandoning their cart due to shipping costs.

6. **Additional Marketing Tool:** Promoting free shipping on your website, social media, or other marketing channels can help attract new customers and drive sales.

Overall, offering free shipping for customers who spend a certain amount can be a powerful marketing tool for eCommerce stores. It can increase sales, improve customer loyalty, and give businesses a competitive edge in the marketplace.

EASY CHECKOUT PROCESS

Picture this: You're shopping online, and you've finally found that perfect gift for a friend. You're ready to checkout and complete your purchase, but the process is so complicated that you end up abandoning your cart and feeling frustrated. Don't lose potential customers because of a confusing checkout process!

An easy checkout process on your eCommerce website is crucial for customer satisfaction and ultimately, sales. Nobody likes a complicated and lengthy checkout process.

By making your checkout process as easy as possible, you're making it easier for customers to complete their purchase. Have you ever heard of the **KISS** principle? **Keep It Simple, Stupid!** Don't overcomplicate things.

So, make sure your checkout process is a breeze! It's a small investment that can pay off big time in customer satisfaction, repeat business, and your bottom line. Let your customers know that you value their time and convenience, and they'll reward you with their loyalty.

Here are seven tips to help you create a clear and easy-to-understand checkout process:

1. **Streamline the checkout process:** Make the checkout process as simple and easy as possible. Reduce the number of steps required to complete the checkout process, eliminate unnecessary fields, and make sure that the process is intuitive and easy to navigate.

2. **Use clear and concise language:** Use language that is easy to understand, clear, and concise. Avoid technical jargon and confusing terminology. Your customers should be able to understand what they need to do at each step of the checkout process.

3. **Provide clear and visible pricing:** Make sure that the pricing is clear and visible throughout the checkout process. This includes showing the price of each item, any taxes or fees, and the total cost of the order.

4. **Offer multiple payment options:** Offer a variety of payment options, such as credit cards, PayPal, and other popular payment methods. This can help to increase the chances of a successful checkout and reduce cart abandonment rates.

5. **Use trust badges and security icons:** Display trust badges and security icons throughout the checkout process to reassure your customers that their personal and financial information is secure.

6. **Enable guest checkout:** Enable guest checkout to allow customers to checkout without creating an account. This can help to reduce friction in the checkout process and increase conversions.

7. **Provide real-time shipping information:** Provide real-time shipping information so that customers can see when their order will arrive. This can help to reduce customer anxiety and increase customer satisfaction.

In conclusion, creating a clear and easy-to-understand checkout process is essential to the success of your eCommerce business. By streamlining the checkout process, using clear and concise language, providing visible pricing, offering multiple payment options, displaying trust badges and security icons, enabling guest checkout, and providing real-time shipping information, you can help to improve the customer experience, reduce cart abandonment rates, and increase conversions.

DETAILED PRODUCT INFORMATION

Provide detailed product information and specifications to help customers make informed decisions. Writing an excellent product description is essential to attract customers and increase sales on an eCommerce website. Remember, unlike shipping in the real world, your customer can't touch or feel your product if it's online. So, your product page must have as much detail as possible.

Here are 13 tips on how to write the perfect product description:

1. **Know your audience:** Before writing a product description, it's important to know who your target audience is. This will help you understand what they are looking for in a product and how to communicate with them effectively.

2. **Use clear and concise language:** Use language that is easy to understand and avoids technical jargon. Use bullet points and short sentences to break up long paragraphs.

3. **Highlight the benefits:** Don't just describe the features of your product, but also highlight how it will benefit the customer. Use descriptive language to paint a picture of how the product will improve their life or solve a problem.

4. **Include high-quality images:** Providing high-quality images of your products can help customers get a better idea of what they are purchasing. Make sure to include multiple angles and zoomed-in shots of any important features or details.

5. **Use bullet points:** Use bullet points to break up the information and make it easier to read and digest. This can also help customers quickly find the information they are looking for.

6. **List product specifications:** List all relevant product specifications, including dimensions, materials, weight, and any other relevant details. This can help customers determine if the product will meet their needs.

7. **Create a sense of urgency:** Use language that creates a sense of urgency and encourages customers to take action. Use phrases like "limited time offer" or "only a few left in stock" to create urgency.

8. **Use social proof:** Including customer reviews and ratings can provide valuable insight into the product and its performance. This can also help build trust and credibility with potential customers.

9. **Use SEO keywords:** Incorporating relevant SEO keywords into your product descriptions can help improve your search engine rankings and drive more traffic to your site.

10. **Be honest and transparent:** Be honest about the product's limitations and potential downsides. This will help build trust with customers and reduce the likelihood of returns or negative reviews.

11. **Provide comparison charts:** If you offer multiple products within the same category, provide a comparison chart to help customers easily compare features and specifications.

12. **Offer video demonstrations:** Video demonstrations can help customers see the product in action and get a better understanding of how it works.

13. **Test and refine:** Continuously test and refine your product descriptions to see what works best and what can be improved. Analyze customer feedback and adjust your descriptions accordingly.

In summary, writing the perfect product description requires a deep understanding of your audience, clear and concise language, highlighting benefits, using high-quality images, including specifications, creating urgency, using social proof, using SEO keywords, being honest and transparent, and continuously testing and refining your descriptions.

HIGH-QUALITY PRODUCT IMAGES

Do you ever find yourself scrolling through eCommerce websites and feeling frustrated by low-quality product images? You're not alone! That's why it's crucial for eCommerce websites to have high-quality product images, and here's why:

Firstly, high-quality product images help customers visualize the product they're interested in. When a product is displayed with crisp, clear images from various angles, it can help customers to get a better idea of what the product looks like in real life. This can increase their confidence in making a purchase and reduce the likelihood of returns or negative reviews.

Secondly, high-quality product images can help to set your business apart from the competition. In a crowded eCommerce market, high-quality images can make your products stand out and catch the eye of potential customers.

Thirdly, high-quality images can also help to build trust with your customers. When customers see that your website features high-quality images, it sends a message that your business is professional and trustworthy.

In addition, high-quality product images can also be a powerful marketing tool. Social media platforms like Instagram and Pinterest are visual platforms, and high-quality product images can help to attract new customers and drive sales.

So, what makes a high-quality product image? It should be well-lit, in focus, and show the product from multiple angles. It's also important to display the product against a clean and neutral background, to avoid any distractions from the product itself.

In short, high-quality product images are a must-have for any eCommerce website. They help customers visualize the product, set your business apart from the competition, build trust, and serve as a powerful marketing tool. So, invest in high-quality product images, and watch your sales soar!

PRODUCT VIDEOS

Using videos and tutorials to highlight your products and how to use them can be an effective way to engage your audience and increase sales on your eCommerce website. Videos can help customers understand the features and benefits of your products in a more dynamic and engaging way than written descriptions alone. Tutorials can also provide valuable information on how to use and maintain the products.

Here are some tips on how to use videos and tutorials effectively to highlight your products:

1. Use high-quality videos: Ensure that the videos are high quality, with good lighting, clear audio, and a professional look and feel. Poor-quality videos can detract from the value of your products and your brand.

2. Highlight the features and benefits: In your videos, be sure to highlight the key features and benefits of your products. This can help customers understand what makes your products unique and why they should buy from you.

3. Keep it concise: Attention spans are short, so keep your videos short and to the point. Focus on the key features and benefits of your products and avoid getting too technical or detailed.

4. Include customer testimonials: Including customer testimonials in your videos can be a powerful way to build trust and credibility with your audience. Hearing from satisfied customers can help potential customers feel more confident about making a purchase.

5. Show how to use the product: Tutorials can be an effective way to demonstrate how to use and maintain your products. This can help customers feel more confident about their purchases and reduce the likelihood of returns or customer service inquiries.

6. Provide links to the product page: Be sure to include links to the product page in your videos and tutorials, so customers can easily find and purchase the products in which they are interested.

In addition to using videos and tutorials on your website, you can also share them on social media and other marketing channels to reach a wider audience. With the right approach, videos and tutorials can be powerful tools to showcase your products, engage your audience, and increase sales on your eCommerce website.

PROVIDE EXCELLENT CUSTOMER SERVICE

By this stage, you have found your product, created an excellent website, and started to get traffic and sales. Now, it's time to think about customer service. This part is crucial, it's what can make or break a business.

In the world of eCommerce, providing top-notch customer service is crucial. It's the glue that holds everything together. Without it, you risk losing customers and damaging your brand's reputation. But with great customer service, you can build loyal customers who keep coming back for more.

Let's break it down. Excellent customer service means providing timely and helpful responses to customer inquiries, ensuring quick and hassle-free delivery, and going above and beyond to address any issues or concerns that customers may have. It's all about creating a seamless shopping experience for your customers, from start to finish.

When customers feel valued and heard, they're more likely to leave positive reviews and refer others to your brand. Plus, providing excellent customer service can also lead to increased sales and revenue. It's a win-win situation.

Some important things to consider when developing your customer service strategy are.

1. **Live chat:** Many eCommerce platforms offer live chat functionality, allowing customers to communicate with support agents in real time. Live chat is a popular option because it allows customers to get immediate help without having to wait on hold or send an email. It is also a convenient option for customers who may be browsing your website outside of business hours.

2. **Email:** Email is a traditional but effective channel for customer support. Many customers prefer to communicate via email because it allows them to explain their issues in detail and attach any relevant screenshots or files. Email is also a good option for more complex issues that may require multiple exchanges.

3. **Phone:** Offering phone support is another essential channel for providing excellent customer service. Phone support allows customers to speak directly with a support agent and get immediate assistance. It is also a good option for customers who may not be comfortable using live chat or email.

4. **Social media:** Many customers use social media to communicate with businesses, so it's important to have a strong social media presence and respond promptly to customer inquiries. You can use social media platforms like Facebook, Twitter, and Instagram to answer customer questions, address concerns, and provide support.

Here are some tips for providing excellent customer service through multiple channels:

1. **Be responsive:** Respond to customer inquiries promptly, even if you can't provide an immediate solution. Let customers know that you're working on their issues and keep them updated throughout the process.

2. **Be friendly and professional:** Always maintain a friendly and professional tone in your communications with customers. Use polite and respectful language and avoid being defensive or confrontational.

3. **Use templates and scripts:** Use pre-written templates and scripts for common customer inquiries to save time and ensure consistency in your responses.

4. **Train your support team:** Make sure your support team is well-trained on your products, policies, and procedures. Provide ongoing training to ensure they have the knowledge and skills to manage a wide range of customer inquiries.

5. **Monitor customer feedback:** Monitor customer feedback and use it to improve your customer service. Pay attention to customer complaints and suggestions and make changes to address any issues or concerns.

In summary, providing excellent customer service through multiple channels is an essential part of running a successful eCommerce business. By offering live chat, email, phone, and social media support, you can ensure that your customers can get the help they need when they need it. Make sure your support team is well-trained and use customer feedback to continually improve your customer service.

LIVE CHAT FOR REAL-TIME SUPPORT

Live chat is a real-time communication feature on a website that enables visitors to interact with customer service representatives or sales representatives of a business instantly. It allows visitors to ask questions, get assistance, and receive support without leaving the website. Live chat is commonly used by businesses to improve customer satisfaction, generate leads, and increase sales.

Live chat involves the use of chat software installed on a website that provides a chat window for visitors to engage with customer service representatives or sales representatives. Visitors can initiate a chat by clicking on a chat icon or button placed on the website, which opens a chat window. They can then type their queries or concerns, and the representative on the other end can respond immediately.

Live chat is a useful tool for businesses because it offers several benefits. Firstly, it provides a quick and convenient way for visitors to get help or support, reducing the need for them to call or email the business. This saves time and effort for both the visitor and the business. Secondly, live chat enables businesses to offer 24/7 customer support, improving customer satisfaction and retention. Thirdly, live chat can increase sales by enabling representatives to assist visitors with product selection, provide recommendations, and address concerns or objections in real-time.

To implement live chat on an eCommerce website, businesses can follow these steps:

1. **Choose a live chat software provider:** There are various live chat software providers available, each with its own features and pricing plans. It is important to choose a provider that offers the features and pricing that best suit the business's needs.

2. **Install the live chat software on the website:** Once the software provider is chosen, the next step is to install the live chat software on the website. This involves adding a code snippet to the website's HTML code, which enables the chat window to appear.

3. **Customize the chat window:** The chat window's appearance can be customized to match the website's branding and design. This includes choosing colors, adding a logo, and setting up pre-chat and post-chat surveys.

4. **Train representatives:** Representatives who will be using the live chat feature should be trained on how to use the software, how to respond to queries and concerns, and how to provide excellent customer service.

5. **Set up automated messages:** Automated messages can be set up to greet visitors when they initiate a chat, or when they are browsing the website for a certain amount of time. These messages can provide a personalized experience for visitors and encourage them to engage with your business.

6. **Monitor and optimize:** The live chat feature should be monitored regularly to ensure that representatives are responding promptly and effectively to visitor queries and concerns. Analytics can also be used to optimize the feature, such as by tracking conversion rates and improving response times.

There are numerous live chat software providers available in the market, but here are five popular options:

1. **LiveChat:** LiveChat is a popular live chat software used by many businesses. It allows you to chat with customers in real time and offers a range of features such as chat transcripts, visitor tracking, and chat ratings.

2. **Zendesk Chat:** Zendesk Chat is a cloud-based live chat software that offers seamless integration with other Zendesk products. It has a range of features, including proactive chat, chat history, and visitor tracking.

3. **Intercom:** Intercom is a customer messaging platform that offers live chat as one of its features. It allows businesses to engage with

customers in real time and offers features such as auto-messages, chatbots, and user segmentation.

4. **Drift:** Drift is a conversational marketing platform that offers live chat, chatbots, and email marketing. It provides real-time engagement with customers and has features such as chat targeting, lead routing, and chat transcripts.

5. **Olark:** Olark is a simple and easy-to-use live chat software that offers features such as chat history, visitor insights, and chat ratings. It also integrates with a range of third-party apps and services.

These are just a few examples of the many live chat software providers available in the market. When choosing a live chat software, it's important to consider factors such as pricing, features, ease of use, and customer support.

In conclusion, live chat is a valuable tool for businesses to improve customer satisfaction, generate leads, and increase sales. Implementing live chat on an eCommerce website involves choosing a software provider, installing the software on the website, customizing the chat window, training representatives, setting up automated messages, and monitoring and optimizing the feature regularly.

CHATBOTS FOR 24/7 SUPPORT

Whilst live chat is perfect for that personal touch, and building customer relationships, chatbots have become increasingly popular in recent years as a means of providing efficient and effective customer support. By using chatbots, eCommerce businesses can offer 24/7 customer support without the need for human staff to be always available. Here are some ways to use chatbots for your eCommerce business:

1. **Integrate chatbots into your website or messaging platforms:** Depending on your business, you may have different messaging platforms such as Facebook Messenger, WhatsApp, or even SMS. You can integrate chatbots into these platforms to provide automated responses to customer inquiries. By having a chatbot readily available to assist customers, you can improve response times and reduce the workload of your customer service team.

2. **Use chatbots to answer frequently asked questions:** By analyzing customer inquiries, you can identify frequently asked questions that

can be answered with a chatbot. You can program your chatbot to respond to these questions with pre-written answers, freeing up your customer service team to focus on more complex inquiries.

3. **Offer personalized recommendations:** By analyzing customer purchase history and behavior, you can program your chatbot to offer personalized product recommendations to customers. This can help increase sales and improve customer satisfaction.

4. **Provide order status updates:** Customers often want to know the status of their orders. You can program your chatbot to provide real-time updates on order status, shipping, and delivery.

5. **Use chatbots to offer promotions and discounts:** By using chatbots, you can offer personalized promotions and discounts to customers based on their purchase history or behavior. This can help increase sales and improve customer loyalty.

6. **Use chatbots to collect customer feedback:** By using chatbots, you can collect feedback from customers about their experiences with your business. This can help you identify areas for improvement and make data-driven decisions.

Overall, chatbots can be a valuable tool for eCommerce businesses to provide efficient and effective customer support, offer personalized recommendations, and collect feedback from customers. By using chatbots, you can improve customer satisfaction, increase sales, and reduce the workload of your customer service team.

CUSTOMER REVIEWS ON WEBSITE

Make it easy for customers to leave reviews and ratings on your website. It is important to make it easy for customers to leave reviews and ratings on your eCommerce website because of the following reasons:

1. **Builds credibility and trust:** Reviews and ratings provide social proof to potential customers, helping them make informed purchase decisions. Positive reviews and high ratings indicate that previous customers have had a good experience with your brand, making it more likely for new customers to trust and do business with you.

2. **Improves search engine ranking:** Search engines like Google consider customer reviews and ratings when ranking websites in search results. Having a high volume of positive reviews can boost your website's ranking and visibility, making it easier for potential customers to find your business.

3. **Increases conversion rates:** Positive reviews and high ratings can significantly increase your conversion rates. According to a study by Spiegel Research Center, products with five reviews have a conversion rate of 270% higher than products with no reviews.

4. **Provides feedback for improvement:** Negative reviews and low ratings can provide valuable feedback for improving your products, services, and customer experience. By listening to customer feedback and addressing their concerns, you can improve your brand's reputation and customer loyalty.

5. **Enhances customer engagement:** Allowing customers to leave reviews and ratings on your eCommerce website creates a sense of community and engagement. Responding to reviews and engaging with customers can also help build stronger relationships and loyalty with your audience.

Overall, making it easy for customers to leave reviews and ratings on your eCommerce website is an important aspect of building trust, improving search engine rankings, increasing conversion rates, receiving valuable feedback, and enhancing customer engagement.

SEARCH ENGINE OPTIMIZATION

Search Engine Optimization (SEO) is a huge subject that encompasses everything from the content on your site, to the content on external sites that link to your website, as well as how your website is coded. However, there are some basic SEO tactics that eCommerce websites should start with to improve their search visibility in Google. Here are some of the most effective strategies:

1. **Optimize product pages:** Use descriptive and unique product titles and descriptions with relevant keywords. Make sure each product page has a unique URL, meta description, and header tags.

2. **Focus on user experience:** Make sure your website is easy to navigate and that your pages load quickly. Provide clear calls to action to encourage visitors to make a purchase.

3. **Use keyword research:** Use keyword research to identify the most relevant and effective keywords for your products and target audience. Incorporate these keywords throughout your website in a natural and organic way.

4. **Optimize for mobile:** Make sure your website is optimized for mobile devices, as more and more people are shopping on their phones and tablets.

5. **Build quality backlinks:** Build quality backlinks to your website from reputable and relevant sources. This can help increase your website's authority and improve your search engine rankings.

6. **Use structured data:** Use structured data to provide additional information about your products, such as price, availability, and reviews. This can help your products stand out in search engine results.

7. **Monitor your website's analytics:** Use website analytics tools to monitor your website's performance, track visitor behavior, and identify areas for improvement.

8. **Content is king:** Keeping your site constantly updated with fresh new, and relevant content is the best way to achieve good results. Your goal should be to answer your customer's questions in the content that you produce.

By using these tactics, eCommerce websites can improve their search visibility in Google, attract more traffic to their website, and increase sales. It's important to remember that SEO is an ongoing process and requires consistent effort and attention to see results over time.

FREE SAMPLES AND TRIALS

Offering free samples and trials is a fantastic way for eCommerce brands to encourage customers to try their products. Here's how and why it works:

1. **Build trust and credibility:** Offering free samples and trials can help build trust and credibility with potential customers. By giving them the opportunity to try your product before committing to a purchase, they can evaluate the quality of the product and decide if it's right for them.

2. **Generate word-of-mouth marketing:** When customers try your product and have a positive experience, they are likely to tell others about it. This can generate valuable word-of-mouth marketing for your brand, which can lead to new customers and increased sales.

3. **Increase conversions:** Offering free samples and trials can increase conversions by giving customers a low-risk way to try your product. Once they have tried it and see the value in it, they are more likely to make a purchase.

4. **Gather feedback:** When customers try your product through a free sample or trial, you have the opportunity to gather feedback from them. This feedback can be used to improve the product and make it more appealing to potential customers.

5. **Showcase new products:** If you have a new product that you want to introduce to the market, offering free samples or trials can be an effective way to generate interest and awareness.

So how can eCommerce brands offer free samples and trials? Here are a few ideas:

1. **Offer free samples with purchase:** When a customer makes a purchase, offer them a free sample of another product in your line. This gives them the opportunity to try something new and may encourage them to make a future purchase.

2. **Provide free trials:** Offer a free trial of your product for a limited time. This can be particularly effective for subscription-based services, as it gives customers the opportunity to try before they commit to a recurring charge.

3. **Host product giveaways:** Host a giveaway on social media or through your email list, offering a certain number of free samples to randomly selected winners.

4. **Partner with influencers:** Partner with influencers in your industry to offer free samples or trials to their followers. This can generate buzz and interest in your product among a relevant audience.

When offering free samples and trials, it's important to be clear about the terms and conditions. Clearly state what the customer is receiving, how long the offer is valid, and any restrictions or limitations. Additionally, make sure to follow up with customers who have tried your product to gather feedback and encourage future purchases.

USE GOOGLE MY BUSINESS

Use Google My Business to boost your local search presence and attract more customers. Google My Business is a free tool that allows businesses to manage their online presence across Google, including search and maps. It is an essential tool for local businesses that want to increase their visibility in local search results and attract more customers.

Here are some steps to use Google My Business to boost your local search presence:

1. **Claim your listing:** The first step is to claim your business listing on Google My Business. If your business is already listed, you can claim it by verifying your ownership. If it is not listed, you can create a new listing.

2. **Optimize your listing:** Once you have claimed your listing, you need to optimize it to make it more appealing to customers. Add photos, videos, business hours, contact information, and a description of your business.

3. **Keep your information up to date:** Make sure your information is accurate and up to date. This includes your address, phone number, and business hours. If you have any changes, make sure to update them on Google My Business.

4. **Encourage customer reviews:** Encourage your customers to leave reviews on Google My Business. Positive reviews can help you attract more customers, while negative reviews can provide valuable feedback for improvement.

5. **Use Google Posts:** Google Posts allows you to share information about your business, such as upcoming events, promotions, and new products. Use this feature to keep your customers updated and engaged.

6. **Monitor your insights:** Google My Business provides valuable insights into how customers are finding and interacting with your business. Monitor these insights to track your performance and identify areas for improvement.

7. **Respond to customer reviews:** Respond to customer reviews, both positive and negative. This shows that you value customer feedback and are committed to providing excellent customer service.

8. **Use Google Maps:** Make sure your business is listed on Google Maps. This allows customers to easily find your business and get directions.

Overall, using Google My Business can help you increase your visibility in local search results and attract more customers to your business. By optimizing your listing, encouraging customer reviews, and monitoring your insights, you can improve your online presence and grow your business.

INVEST IN PAID ADVERTISING

Running paid advertising campaigns on social media and search engines can help your eCommerce business increase its visibility, generate targeted traffic, drive immediate results, track and measure ROI, and gain a competitive advantage. By incorporating paid advertising into your overall marketing strategy, you can achieve greater success and growth for your eCommerce business.

Here are just a few reasons why it is important to run paid advertising campaigns.

1. **Increased visibility:** Paid advertising can increase your eCommerce business's visibility and reach a wider audience than organic methods alone. This can help you generate more traffic to your website and increase your brand awareness.

2. **Targeted advertising:** Paid advertising allows you to target specific demographics, interests, behaviors, and geographic locations. This means that you can reach the people who are most likely to be interested in your products, which can increase your chances of making a sale.

3. **Immediate results:** Unlike organic methods such as search engine optimization (SEO) and content marketing, paid advertising can deliver immediate results. This means that you can start generating traffic and sales as soon as your advertising campaign goes live.

4. **Measurable ROI:** Paid advertising allows you to track and measure your return on investment (ROI) in real time. This means that you can see exactly how much you're spending on advertising and how much revenue it's generating for your eCommerce business.

5. **Competitive advantage:** Running paid advertising campaigns can give you a competitive advantage over other eCommerce businesses in your industry. By reaching your target audience with targeted advertising, you can increase your market share and drive more sales than your competitors.

Here are some tips for running successful paid advertising campaigns on social media and search engines:

1. **Define your target audience:** Before launching any paid advertising campaign, it's important to define your target audience. Consider demographics such as age, gender, location, and interests. Use this information to target your advertising to the right audience.

2. **Choose the right platform:** Different social media platforms and search engines have different advertising options and audiences. Choose the platform that best aligns with your target audience and advertising goals.

3. **Set your advertising budget:** Set a clear advertising budget based on your business goals and the estimated cost per click (CPC) or cost per impression (CPM) for your target audience and platform.

4. **Choose your advertising format:** Social media platforms and search engines offer different advertising formats, such as text ads, display ads, and video ads. Choose the format that aligns with your advertising goals and resonates with your target audience.

5. **Create compelling ad copy:** Your ad copy should be engaging, informative, and relevant to your target audience. Use clear calls-to-action and compelling language to encourage clicks and conversions.

6. **Design eye-catching visuals:** Visuals can make or break your advertising campaign. Use high-quality images or videos that showcase your products and capture the attention of your target audience.

7. **Use targeting options:** Social media platforms and search engines offer various targeting options, such as location, demographics, interests, behaviors, and remarketing. Use these targeting options to reach your ideal audience and increase the effectiveness of your advertising campaign.

8. **Optimize your landing pages:** Your landing page is the first page your visitors will see after clicking on your ad. Ensure that your landing page is optimized for conversions and aligns with the messaging and visuals of your advertising campaign.

9. **Track and measure your results:** Use tracking and measurement tools to monitor the performance of your advertising campaigns. Analyze metrics such as click-through rates (CTR), conversion rates, and return on ad spend (ROAS). Use this data to optimize your campaigns and improve your results.

10. **A/B test your campaigns:** A/B testing involves creating multiple variations of your advertising campaigns and comparing their performance. Test different ad copy, visuals, targeting options, and landing pages to identify what works best for your target audience.

In summary, running paid advertising campaigns on social media and search engines can be a powerful way to promote your eCommerce brand and drive sales. To run a successful paid advertising campaign, define your target audience, choose the right platform, set your budget, choose your advertising format, create compelling ad copy, design eye-catching visuals, use targeting options, optimize your landing pages, track and measure your results, and A/B test your campaigns. By following these tips, you can create effective paid advertising campaigns that drive traffic, conversions, and revenue for your eCommerce business.

USE GOOGLE SHOPPING

From a business owner's perspective, Google Shopping is a powerful tool that can help increase brand visibility and drive sales. By listing your products on Google Shopping, you're essentially putting them in front of millions of potential customers who are actively searching for the products you offer.

One of the benefits of Google Shopping is that it's a cost-effective advertising platform. Unlike traditional advertising methods where you pay for clicks or impressions, with Google Shopping, you only pay when a shopper clicks on your product listing. This means you're not wasting money on ads that aren't generating any clicks or sales.

Google Shopping requires some effort on your part. You'll need to create a product feed, optimize your product listings, and set up a Google Ads account to start advertising. But once you have everything set up, you can start reaping the rewards of increased brand visibility, traffic, and sales.

Using Google Shopping can be extremely beneficial for eCommerce businesses for three main reasons:

1. **Increased Visibility:** By listing your products on Google Shopping, you increase your visibility in Google search results. This means that potential customers are more likely to see your products when they search for relevant keywords.

2. **Higher Quality Traffic:** Google Shopping typically attracts higher quality traffic than other channels, such as social media advertising. This is because shoppers who use Google Shopping are often further along in the buying process and are more likely to convert.

3. **Better ROI:** Google Shopping can be a cost-effective advertising option, especially for smaller eCommerce businesses. Because you only pay when someone clicks on your product listing, you can ensure that you are only paying for relevant traffic.

So, how do you use Google Shopping to showcase your products and reach more customers? Here are the steps you need to follow:

1. **Set up a Google Merchant Center Account:** To list your products on Google Shopping, you first need to set up a Google Merchant Center account. This will allow you to upload your product data and manage your product listings.

2. **Create a Product Feed:** Once you have set up your Google Merchant Center account, you need to create a product feed. This is a file that contains information about your products, such as the title, description, price, and image. You can create your product feed manually or use a tool to automate the process. Some platforms, such as Shopify provide apps/plugins that connect to your Google account and update your product feed automatically.

3. **Link Your Google Ads Account:** Next, you need to link your Google Merchant Center account to your Google Ads account. This will allow you to create shopping campaigns and advertise your products on Google.

4. **Create a Shopping Campaign:** Once your accounts are linked, you can create a shopping campaign. This involves setting a budget, selecting the products you want to advertise, and choosing your target audience.

5. **Optimize Your Product Data:** To ensure that your products appear in relevant search results, you need to optimize your product data. This means using keywords in your product titles and descriptions, providing accurate product information, and ensuring that your product images are high quality.

6. **Monitor and Adjust Your Campaign:** Finally, it is important to monitor your campaign and adjust your strategy as needed. This involves tracking your performance metrics, such as click-through rates and conversion rates, and making changes to your targeting or bidding strategy as needed.

Overall, Google Shopping is a valuable marketing tool that can help businesses of all sizes reach more customers and drive more sales. By leveraging its powerful features and optimization tools, business owners can achieve greater success in the competitive world of eCommerce.

USE RETARGETING ADVERTISING

eCommerce retargeting advertising is a form of digital advertising that targets people who have previously visited your website but did not make a purchase. Retargeting advertising uses cookies to track website visitors and show them targeted ads on other websites or social media platforms.

The goal of retargeting is to remind potential customers of products they were interested in and encourage them to return to your website to complete a purchase. Retargeting ads can be highly effective because they are targeted to people who have already shown an interest in your products, making them more likely to convert into paying customers.

Retargeting ads can be displayed in a variety of formats, including display ads, social media ads, and even email marketing. By showing potential customers relevant products and offers, retargeting advertising can help increase sales, improve customer loyalty, and drive overall revenue for your businesses.

Here are some tips on how to use retargeting ads to effectively reach these customers:

1. **Identify your audience:** Use website analytics to identify the customers who have shown interest in your products. This can include customers who have viewed a product page, added a product to their cart, or visited your website multiple times.

2. **Create relevant ads:** Create ads that are relevant to the specific products or pages that the customer has viewed. This can include product images, descriptions, and pricing information.

3. **Use compelling language:** Use language that is compelling and encourages the customer to take action, such as "Limited Time Offer" or "Free Shipping".

4. **Offer incentives:** Offer incentives such as discounts or free shipping to encourage the customer to make a purchase.

5. **Use frequency capping:** Use frequency capping to limit the number of times the customer sees the retargeting ad. This can prevent the customer from feeling overwhelmed or annoyed by the ad.

6. **Use a variety of ad formats:** Use a variety of ad formats, such as display ads, video ads, or social media ads, to reach customers on different platforms.

7. **Measure your results:** Use analytics tools to measure the effectiveness of your retargeting ads, such as click-through rates, conversion rates, and return on ad spend.

Overall, Google Shopping is a valuable marketing tool that can help businesses of all sizes reach more customers and drive more sales. By leveraging its powerful features and optimization tools, business owners can achieve greater success in the competitive world of eCommerce.

USE REMARKETING CAMPAIGNS

Remarketing and retargeting are two terms that are often used interchangeably, but they refer to different marketing strategies.

Remarketing is a marketing strategy that targets people who have already interacted with your brand or website in some way, such as by visiting your site, filling out a form, or making a purchase. The goal of remarketing is to keep your brand top-of-mind and encourage these previous visitors to come back and engage with your brand again. Remarketing campaigns can be run across different channels, such as email, social media, and display advertising.

Retargeting, on the other hand, refers to a distinct form of remarketing that focuses on individuals who have previously visited your website but failed to perform a specific desired action, such as purchasing a product or submitting a form.

The goal with remarketing is to entice users to return to your website to finalize their transaction. A popular and very important remarketing strategy is abandoned basket email campaigns.

Abandoned basket email campaigns are a type of remarketing strategy that targets customers who have added items to their shopping cart but didn't complete the checkout process. These campaigns involve sending targeted emails to these customers with the goal of encouraging them to come back and complete their purchase.

The idea behind abandoned basket email campaigns is that many customers may have added items to their cart with the intention of buying them, but for various reasons, such as distractions or interruptions, they didn't complete the purchase. By sending a reminder email, you can bring their attention back to the items they were interested in and prompt them to take action.

To create an effective abandoned basket email campaign, there are a few key elements to consider. First, the email should be timely, ideally sent within a few hours of the customer abandoning their cart – I personally always set mine campaigns to send after 60 minutes. This helps keep the items top-of-mind and increases the chances of the customer returning to complete the purchase.

The email should also be personalized and targeted to the specific items in the customer's cart. This can be achieved by including product images, descriptions, and pricing information in the email. You can also use dynamic content to display related products or promotions that may be of interest to the customer.

Another important element is the call-to-action (CTA) in the email. The CTA should be clear, prominent, and encourage the customer to return to their cart and complete the purchase. You can also offer incentives, such as free shipping or a discount code, to entice the customer to complete their purchase.

Here are some steps to manage email campaigns for abandoned baskets:

1. **Collect customer email addresses:** To manage email campaigns for abandoned baskets, you need to collect customer email addresses when they abandon their shopping carts. You can do this by asking customers to provide their email address at checkout or by using a pop-up or exit-intent form to collect email addresses.

2. **Set up an email campaign:** Once you have collected customer email addresses, you can set up an email campaign using an email marketing platform like Mailchimp or Constant Contact. This involves creating a targeted email that is designed to encourage customers to return to your website and complete their purchase.

3. **Create a compelling subject line:** The subject line of your email is crucial in getting customers to open your email. Make sure your subject line is clear, concise, and compelling. Use attention-grabbing phrases that highlight the benefits of returning to complete the purchase.

4. **Personalize your message:** Personalization is key when it comes to managing email campaigns for abandoned baskets. Use the customer's name in the email and include a list of the items they left in their basket. You can also offer personalized product recommendations based on their browsing history and purchase behavior.

5. **Offer an incentive:** To further entice customers to return to your website, consider offering them an incentive. This can be in the form of a discount or free shipping. Make sure to communicate the incentive clearly in your email to encourage the customer to take action.

6. **Create a sense of urgency:** To create a sense of urgency, include a deadline for the incentive you are offering. This can motivate customers to take action quickly and complete their purchase before the offer expires.

7. **Test and refine your campaign:** It's important to test and refine your email campaign over time to improve its effectiveness. This can involve experimenting with different subject lines, incentives, and calls to action. Monitor your email open and click-through rates to see how your campaign is performing and make adjustments as needed.

Abandoned basket email campaigns can be a highly effective remarketing strategy, with studies showing that they can lead to significant increases in conversion rates and revenue. By using targeted and personalized emails, you can help bring customers back to your website and encourage them to complete their purchase, ultimately boosting your bottom line. Don't forget to test and refine your campaign over time to optimize its performance and maximize your results.

CREATE PROMOTIONS AND DISCOUNTS

eCommerce promotions and discounts are marketing strategies that businesses use to attract customers and drive sales. By offering discounts, businesses can increase customer loyalty, entice new customers, and clear out inventory. Here are some important aspects to consider when creating eCommerce promotions and discounts:

1. **Types of promotions and discounts:** There are many types of eCommerce promotions and discounts, such as a percentage off, buy one get one free, free shipping, and coupon codes. Each type of promotion can target different customer segments and lead to different outcomes, so it's important to choose the right type of promotion for your business's goals.

2. **Timing:** Timing is crucial when it comes to eCommerce promotions and discounts. You need to choose the right time to offer a promotion to maximize its effectiveness. For example, you could offer a discount during holidays or special events when people are more likely to make purchases.

3. **Target audience:** You should tailor your promotions and discounts to your target audience. Consider the demographics, interests, and buying behavior of your customers to create promotions that appeal to them. For instance, if your customers are price-sensitive, you could offer a percentage off promotion.

4. **Promotion duration:** The duration of a promotion can impact its success. Promotions that are too short may not give customers enough time to make a decision, while promotions that are too long may not create a sense of urgency. You should find the right balance to ensure that the promotion is effective.

5. **Promotion terms and conditions:** It's important to clearly outline the terms and conditions of your promotions and discounts. This helps to avoid confusion and disappointment among customers. For example, you could specify the minimum purchase amount to qualify for a discount or the expiration date of a coupon code.

6. **Tracking and measuring:** To evaluate the success of your promotions and discounts, you need to track and measure the results. You could use analytics tools to track the number of orders, revenue, and customer retention rates. This information can help you adjust your promotions and discounts to maximize their effectiveness.

7. **Brand image:** Your promotions and discounts should align with your brand image and values. You don't want to undermine your brand's reputation by offering promotions that are seen as deceptive or misleading. Be transparent and honest with your promotions and discounts to build trust with your customers.

Benefits of eCommerce Promotions and Discounts:

1. **Increased sales:** Promotions and discounts can increase sales by enticing customers to make purchases they might not have made otherwise.

2. **Improved customer loyalty:** By offering promotions and discounts, businesses can encourage repeat business and build customer loyalty.

3. **Attract new customers:** Promotions and discounts can attract new customers who are looking for a good deal.

4. **Clear inventory:** Promotions and discounts can help businesses clear out inventory, reducing storage costs and freeing up space for new products.

5. **Boost brand awareness:** Promotions and discounts can help businesses increase their brand awareness by reaching a larger audience.

In summary, eCommerce promotions and discounts are powerful marketing tools that can help businesses attract new customers, improve customer loyalty, increase sales, clear inventory, and boost brand awareness. To create effective promotions and discounts, businesses should consider the types of promotions, timing, target audience, promotion duration, promotion terms and conditions, tracking and measuring, and brand image. By carefully planning and executing promotions and discounts, businesses can achieve their goals and enhance their eCommerce operations.

USE SEASONAL PROMOTIONS

Seasonal promotions for an eCommerce brand are marketing strategies that are designed to capitalize on seasonal events or holidays to boost sales and engage with customers. These promotions can be a powerful tool for eCommerce brands to increase their revenue and build brand awareness. Every brand should have a marketing calendar which displays all the various promotions which it could run throughout the year.

Some examples of seasonal promotions include:

1. **Holiday Sales:** Promotions around major holidays like Christmas, Thanksgiving, Halloween, Easter, Valentine's Day, or Mother's Day.

2. **Seasonal Sales:** Promotions focused on specific seasons such as summer, winter, autumn or spring, which can include products or services related to that season.

3. **Back-to-School Sales:** Promotions that target students and parents gearing up for the school year.

4. **Black Friday/Cyber Monday:** Promotions around the weekend after Thanksgiving, where retailers offer discounts and deals to shoppers.

5. **New Year Sales:** Promotions centered around the start of a new year, often including products that align with New Year's resolutions.

6. **Sports Events:** Promotions that take advantage of major sporting events like the Super Bowl, World Cup or Olympics.

7. **Anniversary Sales:** Promotions celebrating a brand's anniversary, which can include limited edition products, giveaways, and discounts.

Here are some tips on how to effectively use seasonal promotions and holiday deals to increase revenue:

1. **Plan ahead:** Start planning your seasonal promotions and holiday deals well in advance. This will give you enough time to create effective marketing campaigns and ensure that your inventory is prepared for the expected increase in sales.

2. **Use a variety of channels:** To reach the widest possible audience, use a variety of marketing channels such as social media, email marketing, and paid advertising.

3. **Create urgency:** Use language that creates a sense of urgency, such as "limited time offer" or "while supplies last" to encourage customers to make a purchase.

4. **Offer free gifts or samples:** Offering a free gift or sample with each purchase can encourage customers to buy more items or make a larger purchase.

5. **Use customer data:** Use data on past purchasing behavior to target customers with personalized offers and promotions. This can increase the likelihood of them making a purchase.

6. **Make it easy for customers:** Make sure your website is easy to navigate and that the checkout process is straightforward. Offer free shipping or expedited shipping to make it even more convenient for customers to shop with you.

7. **Follow up:** Follow up with customers who made a purchase during the seasonal promotion or holiday deal with a thank you email and a special offer for future purchases. This can help to build customer loyalty and encourage repeat business.

By using seasonal promotions and holiday deals effectively, eCommerce stores can increase sales, attract new customers, and build customer loyalty. With careful planning and targeted marketing, these promotions can be a highly effective way to boost revenue and grow your business.

CREATE A LOYALTY PROGRAM

A loyalty program is a marketing strategy that is designed to reward customers for their continued business and encourage them to make repeat purchases. Loyalty programs can take many different forms, but they all aim to incentivize customer loyalty by offering rewards, perks, or other benefits for customers who frequently engage with a business.

For example, a loyalty program for an eCommerce business might offer customers points or credits for each purchase they make, which can be redeemed for discounts, free items, or other rewards. Loyalty programs can also offer other benefits, such as early access to new products, exclusive sales, or free shipping.

The ultimate goal of a loyalty program is to build a long-term relationship between a business and its customers. By offering rewards and other benefits, businesses can encourage customers to continue shopping with them, even when there are other competitors in the market. Loyalty programs also provide businesses with valuable customer data, which can be used to better understand the needs and preferences of their customers.

Some common types of loyalty programs include:

1. **Points-based programs:** Customers earn points for each purchase they make, which can be redeemed for discounts, free items, or other rewards.

2. **Tiered programs:** Customers are assigned to different tiers based on their level of engagement with a business. Each tier offers its own set of rewards and benefits, with higher tiers offering more exclusive perks.

3. **Cash-back programs:** Customers earn a percentage of their purchase back in the form of cash, which can be used to make future purchases.

4. **Coalition programs:** Multiple businesses come together to offer a joint loyalty program, allowing customers to earn and redeem rewards across multiple brands.

Implementing a loyalty program can be a powerful way to increase customer retention, encourage repeat purchases, and build brand loyalty. However, it's important to carefully consider the costs and benefits of a loyalty program before implementing one. A well-designed loyalty program can be a valuable tool for any business, but a poorly designed program can drive customers away.

1. **Determine the type of loyalty program that fits your business:** There are different types of loyalty programs, such as points-based, tiered, and cashback programs. Decide which type fits your business goals and budget.

2. **Choose the rewards:** Decide what rewards you will offer to your loyal customers, such as discounts, free products, free shipping, exclusive access to events or content, or early access to new products.

3. **Set up a point system:** If you opt for a point system, determine the value of each point and how customers can earn them. For example, customers can earn points for making a purchase, sharing products on social media, referring friends, writing reviews, or signing up for your newsletter.

4. **Promote your loyalty program:** Make sure your customers are aware of your loyalty program by promoting it on your website, social media channels, email campaigns, and order confirmation pages. Consider using pop-ups or banners to promote your loyalty program and encourage sign-ups.

5. **Use technology to manage your loyalty program:** Use loyalty program software or an eCommerce platform with built-in loyalty program features to manage and automate the process. This will make it easier to track customer activities, points, and rewards, and send notifications and reminders to customers.

6. **Monitor and optimize your program:** Regularly monitor your loyalty program performance, analyze customer data and feedback, and optimize your program based on the insights you gather. For example, you might need to adjust the rewards, point values, or promotion channels to improve customer engagement and retention.

By implementing a loyalty program, you can create a strong bond with your customers and increase customer lifetime value. It is important to keep in mind that a loyalty program is just one aspect of customer retention, and it should be combined with other strategies such as great customer service, personalized experiences, and engaging content.

CREATE A REFERRAL PROGRAM

Offering a referral program is an effective way to encourage your customers to spread the word about your brand and products. A referral program incentivizes your existing customers to refer their friends, family, or colleagues to your eCommerce store, which can help increase your customer base and sales. In this way, it can be a cost-effective and powerful marketing strategy for your business.

Here are some steps to help you implement a referral program for your eCommerce business:

1. **Define your referral program goals:** Before you start designing your referral program, you need to define your goals. For instance, you may want to increase your customer base, increase your sales, or improve your customer retention. Having clear goals will help you tailor your referral program to achieve those specific objectives.

2. **Choose a referral incentive:** You need to offer a referral incentive to encourage your customers to participate in the program. The incentive could be in the form of a discount, a free product, or store credit. Make sure the incentive is attractive enough to motivate your customers to refer their friends.

3. **Set up your referral program:** You can use referral software to set up your program. Many eCommerce platforms offer plugins and apps that can help you create a referral program quickly and easily. Alternatively, you can use third-party software like ReferralCandy or Ambassador to set up and manage your program.

4. **Promote your referral program:** Once you have set up your referral program, you need to promote it to your customers. You can do this by sending an email to your customer list, posting about it on social media, or displaying a banner on your website. Make sure your customers know about the program and the incentives they can receive.

5. **Monitor your referral program:** It is essential to monitor your referral program's performance regularly. This will help you identify any issues that need to be addressed, such as a low conversion rate or a high churn rate. You can use analytics to track the number of referrals, conversion rates, and revenue generated by the program.

6. **Provide a seamless customer experience:** Make sure your referral program is easy to use and navigate. Customers should be able to refer their friends quickly and easily, without having to jump through hoops. A seamless customer experience will increase the likelihood of customers participating in the program and referring their friends.

In conclusion, a referral program is a great way to attract new customers and increase sales for your eCommerce business. By offering incentives to your existing customers, you can leverage their network to expand your reach and visibility. Implementing a referral program requires careful planning and execution, but the benefits are well worth the effort.

BUILD A STRONG SOCIAL MEDIA PRESENCE

Build a strong social media presence and engage with your followers regularly. In today's digital age, having a strong social media presence is critical for any eCommerce brand that wants to reach a larger audience and build a strong online reputation. Here are some tips for building a strong social media presence for an eCommerce brand:

1. **Choose the right platforms:** Not all social media platforms are created equal, and it's important to choose the right platforms for your brand. Consider your target audience and where they are most active online. For example, if your target audience is young adults, Instagram and TikTok might be more effective than Facebook or LinkedIn.

2. **Develop a social media strategy:** A well-planned social media strategy is essential for building a strong social media presence. Your strategy should define your goals, target audience, content themes, posting frequency, and performance metrics. It should also

111

consider how to engage with your audience and build a community around your brand.

3. **Create high-quality content:** Your social media content should be visually appealing, informative, and relevant to your target audience. Use high-quality images and videos to showcase your products and tell your brand story. Consider creating content themes that align with your brand's values and personality.

4. **Engage with your audience:** Engaging with your audience is essential for building a strong social media presence. Respond to comments, messages, and reviews in a timely manner. Ask questions, encourage user-generated content, and participate in relevant conversations to show your brand's personality and build a community.

5. **Use social media advertising:** Social media advertising can be a powerful tool for reaching a larger audience and promoting your eCommerce brand. Use paid advertising to target specific audiences, promote your products, and drive traffic to your website. Use A/B testing to optimize your ads and maximize their effectiveness.

6. **Leverage influencers:** Influencer marketing can be an effective way to build a strong social media presence for your eCommerce brand. Identify influencers who align with your brand values and target audience, and partner with them to promote your products and increase your brand visibility.

7. **Analyze your performance:** Analyzing your social media performance is essential for identifying what works and what doesn't. Use analytics tools to track engagement, reach, and conversion rates. Use this information to adjust your social media strategy and improve your performance.

In conclusion, building a strong social media presence is essential for any eCommerce brand that wants to increase its online visibility, reach a larger audience, and build a strong online reputation. To build a strong social media presence, brands should choose the right platforms, develop a social media strategy, create high-quality content, engage with their audience, use social media advertising, leverage influencers, and analyze their performance. By following these tips, eCommerce brands can create a powerful social media presence that drives sales and builds brand loyalty.

COLLABORATE WITH BRANDS AND INFLUENCERS

Teaming up with other brands and influencers can be a powerful strategy for eCommerce brands to broaden their exposure and increase their visibility. Through partnerships with other brands and influencers, eCommerce companies can reach a broader audience and draw in fresh customers who might not have been aware of their brand before. Here are a few justifications why eCommerce brands should contemplate joining forces with other brands and influencers:

1. **Reach a new audience:** Partnering with other brands and influencers allows eCommerce businesses to reach a wider audience beyond their existing customer base. By collaborating with influencers who have a large following on social media platforms, eCommerce brands can tap into their followers and attract new customers who may be interested in their products or services.

2. **Build credibility:** Partnering with other brands and influencers can help eCommerce businesses build credibility and trust with their target audience. When an influencer or another reputable brand promotes a product or service, it adds to the brand's credibility and can increase the likelihood of customers purchasing from the brand.

3. **Cost-effective marketing:** Collaborating with other brands and influencers can be a cost-effective way to market an eCommerce business. Instead of spending a lot of money on traditional advertising methods, eCommerce brands can leverage the audience of another brand or influencer without having to spend as much money.

4. **Increase social media presence:** Partnering with influencers who have a large following on social media can help eCommerce businesses increase their social media presence. When an influencer promotes a product or service on social media, it can generate a lot of engagement, likes, and shares, which can increase the visibility of the eCommerce brand.

5. **Create unique content:** Collaborating with other brands and influencers can also help eCommerce businesses create unique and interesting content. By working with other brands and influencers, eCommerce businesses can create content that is more engaging and appealing to their target audience, which can lead to more sales and brand awareness.

There are many ways that you can collaborate with other brands or influencers, it's really limited to the imagination. But here are some examples to give you some ideas.

1. **Co-creation of products:** Create a unique product or collection of products. This allows both parties to bring their expertise and strengths to the collaboration and can result in a unique product that appeals to both brands' audiences.

2. **Influencer marketing:** Partner with influencers to promote your products to their followers. This can include sponsored posts, product reviews, or other types of content that showcase the brand's products and highlight their benefits.

3. **Social media campaigns:** Collaborate with other brands or influencers on social media campaigns that promote a shared message or theme. This can help to increase exposure for both brands and reach a wider audience.

4. **Events and pop-ups:** Collaborate to host events or pop-ups that showcase your products. This can be a great way to generate buzz and excitement around the brand, while also providing a unique experience for customers.

5. **Charitable collaborations:** eCommerce brands can partner with other brands or influencers on charitable collaborations, where a portion of the proceeds from the collaboration go towards a specific cause or charity. This can help to increase the brand's social responsibility and appeal to customers who value socially conscious brands.

6. **Competitions:** Consider teaming up with another brand to run a competition where both of you provide products as prizes. Use social media to promote the competition and attract a wider audience, which can help you to capture more leads and grow your email marketing list.

To give you some more inspiration, here are five examples of how other brands have collaborated.

1. **Nike x Off-White:** Nike teamed up with fashion designer Virgil Abloh's streetwear brand, Off-White, to create a collection of limited-edition sneakers and athletic wear. The collaboration generated buzz and excitement among sneakerheads and fashion enthusiasts, resulting in a sell-out of the products within minutes of release.

2. **Target x Vineyard Vines:** Target partnered with preppy clothing brand Vineyard Vines to launch a limited-edition collection of clothing and accessories. The collaboration allowed Target to tap into Vineyard Vines' affluent customer base while offering the brand's signature styles at a lower price point.

3. **Amazon x Chrissy Teigen:** Amazon teamed up with cookbook author and model Chrissy Teigen to launch an exclusive line of kitchenware and cookbooks. The collaboration leveraged Teigen's celebrity status and social media following to promote the products to her fans, resulting in increased sales for Amazon.

4. **ASOS x GLAAD:** Online fashion retailer ASOS collaborated with LGBTQ+ advocacy organization GLAAD to launch a collection of gender-neutral clothing. The collaboration aimed to promote inclusivity and diversity, and a portion of the proceeds went towards supporting GLAAD's work.

5. **Boohoo x Gemma Collins:** Online fashion retailer Boohoo partnered with reality TV star Gemma Collins to launch a collection of plus-size clothing. The collaboration aimed to offer fashionable clothing options for all sizes and leveraged Collins' popularity to promote the products to her fans.

In conclusion, collaborating with other brands and influencers is an effective way for eCommerce brands to expand their reach and visibility. By partnering with influencers and other reputable brands, eCommerce businesses can reach a wider audience, build credibility, increase their social media presence, and create unique and interesting content.

EMAIL MARKETING

Email marketing is a digital marketing strategy that involves sending promotional messages and newsletters to a targeted list of subscribers. It is a cost-effective and direct way for businesses to reach out to their customers and prospects, with the aim of increasing sales, building brand awareness, and fostering customer loyalty.

It typically involves creating engaging and informative content, such as product updates, industry news, special offers, or educational resources, and delivering it to subscribers via email. The content can be personalized and targeted to specific segments of the email list, based on factors such as past purchase behavior, demographics, or interests.

Campaigns should also include calls-to-action that encourage subscribers to take specific actions, such as making a purchase, visiting a website, or sharing the email with their friends and family. Advanced email marketing platforms can provide detailed analytics and tracking features, which allow businesses to measure the success of their campaigns and optimize their email marketing strategies over time.

Email marketing is a highly effective tool for eCommerce businesses, and it can be relatively inexpensive to implement. Most email marketing software providers charge based on the number of contacts or emails sent per month. If you have a small subscriber list, your costs will likely be low. As you grow your list and invest more in email marketing, you can expect to see a proportional return on investment.

The first step in developing an effective email marketing strategy is to build a high-quality list of subscribers. While other businesses may boast about the size of their lists, it's important to focus on quality over quantity. Your goal should be to attract subscribers who are interested in your content and likely to make purchases from your website. A large list with a low conversion rate is of little value, and a poor-quality list can damage your reputation as a sender. Subscribers who unsubscribe, block, or report your emails can hurt your sender reputation and decrease the likelihood of your emails reaching the inbox instead of the spam folder. Here are some effective methods for building an email subscriber list.

1. **Offer an incentive:** Offer a discount code or other incentive in exchange for signing up to your email list. This encourages visitors to your website to provide their email address and increases the chances they will become a customer.

2. **Opt-in at checkout:** Provide an option for customers to opt-in to your email list during the checkout process. This is an easy way to capture email addresses from those who are already making a purchase on your website.

3. **Create gated content:** Create exclusive content such as eBooks, webinars, or whitepapers and make them available only to those who sign up for your email list. This gives visitors an incentive to sign up and positions your brand as an expert in your industry.

4. **Use social media:** Use your social media channels to promote your email list and encourage followers to sign up. Consider running a social media contest where entering requires subscribing to your email list.

5. **Host events:** Host events such as webinars or in-person events and encourage attendees to sign up for your email list for exclusive updates and offers.

6. **Leverage pop-ups:** Use pop-ups on your website to encourage visitors to sign up for your email list. Be strategic about when the pop-up appears and what incentive is offered to maximize the number of sign-ups.

7. **Run targeted ads:** Use targeted advertising to reach potential subscribers and encourage them to sign up for your email list. Consider using Facebook ads or Google ads to reach a wider audience.

Here are some general tips on how you can improve your email marketing strategy.

1. **Segment your list:** Once you have a list of subscribers, it's important to segment it based on different criteria such as location, purchase history, and interests. This allows you to send targeted emails to specific groups of subscribers that are more likely to be interested in the content or products you're promoting.

2. **Test different subject lines and designs:** A/B split testing functionality is commonly provided by email marketing software providers. I highly recommend utilizing this feature for most of your email campaigns. Crafting an effective subject line is a skill that requires extensive experimentation to determine what resonates with your audience. Having captivating subject lines is crucial for enhancing your email open rates. While testing different designs to improve click-through rates is also valuable, it's best to prioritize subject lines and test them individually before moving on to other aspects.

3. **Choose the right email service provider:** There are many email service providers available that offer a range of features and pricing options. It's important to choose the one that best fits your needs and budget. Some popular options include Mailchimp, Constant Contact, and Campaign Monitor.

4. **Create compelling content:** The content of your email campaigns should be engaging and relevant to your subscribers. This could include new product announcements, exclusive promotions, or helpful content such as how-to guides or industry news. Make sure to include high-quality images and clear calls to action.

5. **Use automation:** Email automation can save you time and help you send more targeted emails. For example, you could set up a welcome email series for new subscribers, abandoned cart emails for customers who left items in their cart, or re-engagement campaigns for subscribers who haven't opened your emails in a while.

6. **Monitor and analyze results:** It's important to track the results of your email campaigns and adjust your strategy accordingly. Look at metrics such as open rates, click-through rates, and conversion rates to see what's working and what's not. You can also use A/B testing to experiment with different subject lines, content, and calls to action.

Try to spend some good quality time on developing your strategy. It will be worth it in the end. There might be a lot of upfront work in the beginning, but if you do it right, you can easily reap the benefits later with a well-structured email marketing strategy. Some other tips to consider are.

- Personalize your emails with the subscriber's name and other relevant information.

- Use clear and concise subject lines that encourage subscribers to open your emails.

- Make sure your emails are mobile-friendly and easy to read on different devices.

- Offer exclusive promotions or discounts to encourage subscribers to make a purchase.

- Don't send too many emails - find the right balance between staying top of mind and overwhelming your subscribers.

Overall, sending newsletters and email campaigns is a powerful tool for eCommerce businesses to drive traffic and sales. By creating compelling content, segmenting your list, using automation, and analyzing your results, you can build a successful email marketing strategy that helps your business grow.

EMAIL MARKETING AUTOMATION

Email marketing automation is the use of software to automate email marketing campaigns. It allows businesses to send targeted and personalized emails to their subscribers based on their behavior and actions on the website or previous interactions with the brand.

Email marketing automation involves setting up workflows that trigger specific email messages based on user behavior, such as signing up for a newsletter, making a purchase, or abandoning a shopping cart. The software can be programmed to send a series of emails, each with a specific purpose, such as welcoming new subscribers, promoting products or services, or nurturing leads.

The main advantage of email marketing automation is that it saves time and effort while allowing businesses to provide a more personalized experience to their subscribers. Instead of manually sending emails to each subscriber, the software does the work automatically, freeing up time for businesses to focus on other tasks. Additionally, email marketing automation allows businesses to send more relevant and timely emails to their subscribers, which can lead to higher engagement and conversion rates.

To use email marketing automation effectively, businesses must first identify their target audience and create a list of subscribers. They can then segment their subscribers based on their interests, behavior, and demographics to send targeted and relevant emails.

When implementing email marketing automation, it's important to follow best practices to ensure that emails are delivered and well received. This includes:

1. **Obtaining permission:** Only send emails to subscribers who have given their consent to receive them.

2. **Personalizing emails:** Use subscribers' names and other information to personalize emails and make them more relevant.

3. **Testing emails:** Test emails before sending them to ensure they are error-free and display correctly on different devices.

4. **Analyzing results:** Monitor email campaign results and use data to optimize future campaigns for better results.

Here are the steps to use email marketing automation to send personalized messages and offers to your customers:

1. **Choose an email marketing automation software:** There are several email marketing automation software providers available, such as Mailchimp, HubSpot, and ActiveCampaign. Choose one that fits your needs and budget.

2. **Set up your automation workflows:** Automation workflows are a series of triggers, actions, and events that define the email campaign's journey. For example, you can set up an automation workflow that triggers an email to be sent when a customer abandons their cart or when they make a purchase.

3. **Segment your email list:** Segmentation is the process of dividing your email list into smaller groups based on specific criteria, such as location, purchase history, or interests. By segmenting your email list, you can send targeted messages and offers to your customers.

4. **Create personalized email content:** Personalized email content is more effective than generic content because it speaks directly to the recipient. Use the customer's name and include personalized product recommendations based on their purchase history or browsing behavior.

5. **Schedule your emails:** Set a schedule for your emails based on the customer's time zone and

behavior. For example, if a customer typically opens your emails in the morning, schedule your emails to be sent at that time.

6. **Test and refine your email campaigns:** Continuously test and refine your email campaigns to optimize their performance. A/B testing is a powerful tool that allows you to compare two different email variations and see which one performs better.

Here are some examples of email marketing automation workflows that you can set up:

1. **Welcome series:** Send a series of welcome emails to new subscribers, introducing them to your brand and products.

2. **Abandoned cart emails:** Send an email to customers who abandoned their shopping cart, reminding them of the items they left behind and offering an incentive to complete their purchase.

3. **Post-purchase emails:** Send a follow-up email to customers who have made a purchase, thanking them for their order and offering a discount code for their next purchase.

4. **Re-engagement emails:** Send a series of re-engagement emails to customers who haven't made a purchase in a while, offering a special incentive or personalized recommendation.

5. **Birthday or anniversary emails:** Send a personalized email to customers on their birthday or anniversary, offering a special discount or free gift.

Overall, email marketing automation can be a powerful tool for eCommerce brands looking to connect with their audience and drive sales. By sending targeted and relevant emails automatically, businesses can save time and provide a more personalized experience for their subscribers.

PERSONALIZED RECOMMENDATIONS AND PRODUCT SUGGESTIONS

For ecommerce businesses, personalized recommendations and product suggestions are game-changing tools that can help increase customer engagement, loyalty, and ultimately revenue.

By leveraging customer data such as browsing history, purchase history, and search queries, businesses can create customized suggestions that cater to individual preferences and needs. These tailored recommendations can improve the overall customer experience, making it easier and more convenient for shoppers to find products they are interested in.

Using techniques such as collaborative filtering and content-based filtering, businesses can analyze customer data to generate personalized recommendations. Collaborative filtering identifies patterns and similarities between customers to suggest products that others with similar tastes have enjoyed. Content-based filtering focuses on the attributes of products to suggest items that match a customer's interests and needs.

The benefits of personalized recommendations and product suggestions extend beyond the customer experience. By providing relevant and timely recommendations, businesses can increase the likelihood of additional purchases, improve customer retention rates, and ultimately boost revenue.

1. **Collect customer data:** The first step to offering personalized product recommendations is to collect customer data. This could include their purchase history, browsing behavior, and demographic information. You can do this by using tools such as Google Analytics, customer surveys, and loyalty programs.

2. **Analyze customer data:** Once you have customer data, you can analyze it to identify patterns and trends. Look for products that customers frequently purchase together, as well as products that customers tend to buy at certain times of the year or in certain categories.

3. **Use recommendation algorithms:** There are many recommendation algorithms available that can analyze customer data and make personalized product recommendations. Some popular options include Collaborative Filtering, Content-Based Filtering, and Hybrid Filtering. These algorithms consider factors such as purchase history, product views, and customer behavior to generate personalized recommendations.

4. **Display personalized recommendations:** Once you have generated personalized product recommendations, you can display them to customers on your website, in email campaigns, and in other marketing channels. Make sure to prominently feature the recommendations and use clear calls to action to encourage customers to make a purchase.

5. **Test and optimize:** It's important to test different types of personalized recommendations and optimize your strategy based on the results. A/B testing can be a powerful tool for this, allowing you to experiment with different types of recommendations and see which ones perform best.

Some tips for offering personalized product recommendations include:

- Start with simple recommendations based on purchase history or product views, and gradually build more complex algorithms as you collect more data.

- Make sure your recommendations are relevant and useful to the customer - avoid recommending products they have already purchased or items that are not in stock.

- Use clear and visually appealing product images and descriptions to showcase the recommended products.

- Don't overwhelm customers with too many recommendations - limit the number of products you display and make sure they are well-organized and easy to navigate.

Overall, offering personalized product recommendations is a powerful way to increase sales and improve customer satisfaction. By collecting customer data, analyzing it, using recommendation algorithms, displaying personalized recommendations, and testing and optimizing your strategy, you can build a successful personalized recommendation system that helps your eCommerce business grow.

USE POP-UPS AND EXIT-INTENT OFFERS

Although we have already mentioned popups in some of the previous sections in this book. It is a powerful tool for lead generation and conversion optimization; therefore, it warrants its own section. Pop-ups and exit-intent offers can be effective ways to capture customers' attention and encourage them to make a purchase on an eCommerce website. Pop-ups are messages or ads that appear on a website, usually in a separate window or box, while exit-intent offers are displayed when a customer is about to leave the website.

Popups are relatively easy to set up. Most email marketing software providers these days provide popup options. And depending on what eCommerce platform you are using, there will be apps or plugins you can install.

Here are some ways to effectively use pop-ups and exit-intent offers:

1. **Offer a discount or promotion:** Customers are often more likely to make a purchase if they feel like they are getting a good deal. Use pop-ups or exit-intent offers to provide customers with a discount code or special promotion that encourages them to complete their purchase.

2. **Provide helpful information:** Use pop-ups or exit-intent offers to provide customers with helpful information, such as product reviews, related items, or sizing guides. This can help to build trust and establish your website as a reliable source of information.

3. **Ask for feedback:** Use pop-ups or exit-intent offers to ask customers for feedback on their shopping experience or their reasons for leaving the website. This can help you to identify areas for improvement and make changes to better meet customers' needs.

4. **Highlight popular products:** Use pop-ups or exit-intent offers to showcase popular or best-selling products. This can help to draw customers' attention to products that are likely to appeal to them and encourage them to make a purchase.

5. **Keep it simple:** Make sure your pop-ups or exit-intent offers are simple and easy to understand. Avoid using complicated language or graphics that may confuse customers or make it difficult for them to complete their purchase.

When using pop-ups or exit-intent offers, it's important to strike a balance between providing helpful information and not overwhelming customers with too many messages or offers. It's also important to make sure that pop-ups and exit-intent offers are optimized for mobile devices, as many customers access websites on their smartphones and tablets.

In addition to these tips, it's important to test different types of pop-ups and exit-intent offers to see what works best for your website and customers. By monitoring the performance of different offers and making data-driven decisions, you can optimize your website to maximize conversions and sales.

UPSELL AND CROSS-SELL YOUR PRODUCTS

Upselling and cross-selling are two effective strategies that online businesses use to increase their average order value and generate more revenue. Upselling refers to encouraging customers to purchase a more expensive version of a product they are interested in or offering them additional items that complement their purchase. Cross-selling, on the other hand, involves suggesting products that are related to or complementary to the customer's purchase.

To offer upselling and cross-selling opportunities, online businesses need to be strategic and considerate in their approach. Here are some tips to effectively implement these tactics:

1. **Analyze customer behavior:** It is essential to understand your customer's purchase history, browsing behavior, and preferences to identify relevant upsell and cross-sell opportunities. You can use tools like Google Analytics, customer surveys, or purchase history data to get insights into what products and categories your customers are interested in.

138

2. **Make relevant product recommendations:** Based on your analysis, you can offer relevant product recommendations to customers at the right time in their buying journey. For instance, you can offer complementary products as customers add items to their cart, or suggest a more premium version of a product they are interested in.

3. **Offer discounts and bundles:** Offering discounts or creating product bundles is another effective way to upsell and cross-sell. For instance, you can offer a discount when a customer purchases a certain quantity of items or creates a bundle of products that complement each other.

4. **Use personalized messages:** Personalized messages can increase the likelihood of a customer making an additional purchase. For example, if a customer has purchased a product from a particular category, you can send them an email or push notification with recommendations for similar products.

5. **Display product recommendations prominently:** Make sure to display your product recommendations prominently on your website or app. You can use pop-ups, banners, or sliders to grab the customer's attention and make it easy for them to add recommended products to their cart.

6. **Test and iterate:** It is essential to test different approaches to upselling and cross-selling to find what works best for your business. You can use A/B testing to try different messaging, offers, and product recommendations to see what resonates best with your customers.

7. **Be transparent and honest:** Customers appreciate honesty and transparency, so make sure your product recommendations are genuine and relevant to their interests. Avoid recommending products that are not related or trying to upsell customers on items that do not fit their budget or needs.

By offering upselling and cross-selling opportunities, online businesses can increase their revenue and provide a better shopping experience for their customers. However, it is important to be strategic and considerate in your approach to ensure that you are providing relevant and valuable recommendations.

CREATE A SENSE OF URGENCY

Scarcity tactics are a set of marketing techniques used in ecommerce to create a sense of urgency and encourage customers to make a purchase. These tactics are based on the principle that people are more likely to buy a product when they perceive it as scarce or in high demand. This can trigger a sense of FOMO (fear of missing out) in customers and prompt them to take action.

One common scarcity tactic used in ecommerce is creating a sense of urgency through time-limited offers, such as flash sales, limited-time discounts, or countdown timers.

Another scarcity tactic is using limited stock or availability to create a sense of scarcity. This can be done by showing the number of items remaining in stock, highlighting that a product is a limited edition or exclusive item, or limiting the availability of a product to specific geographic locations.

Social proof is another technique used to create a sense of scarcity. This tactic involves showing that a product is in high demand by highlighting the number of views, likes, or reviews a product has received. By emphasizing the popularity of a product, businesses can create a sense of urgency and encourage customers to make a purchase before the product sells out.

1. **Limited stock:** One of the most common scarcity tactics is to create a sense of urgency by limiting the number of products available. You can do this by indicating how many items are left in stock or by setting a time limit for the sale. For example, you can display a message such as "Only 5 items left in stock" or "Sale ends in 24 hours."

2. **Limited-time offers:** You can also use limited-time offers to create a sense of urgency. This can be a sale that lasts only for a few hours or a special discount code that expires in a set amount of time. By giving customers a specific deadline to make a purchase, you can motivate them to act quickly.

3. **Exclusive offers:** Creating exclusive offers for your customers is another way to use scarcity tactics. For example, you can offer a special discount code only to your email subscribers or to customers who have previously made a purchase. This makes customers feel valued and encourages them to make a purchase to take advantage of the exclusive offer.

4. **Bundles and packages:** Offering bundles or packages of products is another way to use scarcity tactics. By bundling products together, you can create a sense of urgency and encourage customers to make a purchase. For example, you can offer a "limited time only" package deal that includes several related products at a discounted price.

5. **Countdown timers:** Adding a countdown timer to your website can create a sense of urgency and encourage customers to make a purchase. For example, you can add a countdown timer to your checkout page that displays how much time is left until the sale ends.

The goal of scarcity tactics in ecommerce is to create a sense of urgency and increase the perceived value of a product, making customers more likely to make a purchase. However, it's important to use these tactics ethically and transparently to avoid damaging customer trust or brand reputation.

SOCIAL PROOF BUILD TRUST AND CREDIBILITY

Social proof is a psychological phenomenon that occurs when individuals look at the actions and behaviors of others to determine their own beliefs, attitudes, and actions. This phenomenon is based on the idea that people often rely on the actions and opinions of others to validate their own beliefs and behaviors.

Social proof can take many different forms, including testimonials from satisfied customers, positive reviews on social media platforms or websites, and endorsements from trusted sources. It can also manifest in the form of social influence, where individuals are influenced by the actions and behaviors of others in their social group.

Social proof is particularly important in marketing and advertising, as it can significantly influence consumer behavior. Companies often use social proof to build trust with potential customers and to demonstrate the effectiveness of their products or services.

Overall, social proof is a powerful psychological tool that can be used to influence the attitudes and behaviors of individuals. By understanding this phenomenon, individuals and businesses can leverage the power of social proof to achieve their goals and build trust with their target audience.

Here are some ways eCommerce businesses can use social proof to build trust and credibility with their audience:

1. **Customer reviews:** Encourage customers to leave reviews of your products and display them prominently on your website. Positive reviews can help potential customers feel more confident in their decision to make a purchase.

2. **Testimonials:** Reach out to satisfied customers and ask them to provide a testimonial about their experience with your products or brand. You can then display these testimonials on your website or in your marketing materials.

3. **Social media mentions:** Monitor social media channels for mentions of your brand and products. If customers are posting positive comments or photos, you can share them on your own social media channels or website.

4. **Influencer marketing:** Partner with influencers or industry experts to promote your products. Customers are more likely to trust a recommendation from someone they follow or admire.

5. **Trust badges:** Display trust badges on your website to indicate that your business is legitimate and trustworthy. Some examples of trust badges include security seals, payment provider logos, and awards or certifications.

6. **User-generated content:** Encourage customers to share photos or videos of themselves using your products on social media. You can then feature this user-generated content on your website or in your marketing materials to showcase real-life examples of your products in action.

By using social proof tactics, eCommerce businesses can build trust and credibility with their audience, which can ultimately lead to increased sales and customer loyalty.

GET CUSTOMER FEEDBACK

As a business owner, it is important to continuously seek ways to improve your business. Since customers are the lifeblood of any business, having a thorough understanding of their needs and identifying any shortcomings in your business can be crucial in building a stronger and more successful brand.

The aim is to cater to the desires of your customers, but some business owners are unsure about how to obtain this information. However, the solution is not complex - simply ask your customers directly to gather the information you need.

Exit surveys are a valuable tool for gathering feedback from customers who have just completed an interaction with your business. The purpose of these surveys is to gain insight into the customer's experience and to identify areas where improvements can be made. Here are some reasons why you should use exit surveys and how to make the most of them:

1. **Identify problems:** Exit surveys can help you identify problems that customers encounter during their interactions with your business. By

gathering feedback from customers who have just completed a transaction, you can identify issues that may have been missed during routine customer service monitoring.

2. **Improve customer experience:** By identifying and addressing issues, you can improve the overall customer experience. For example, if a customer indicates that they had difficulty navigating your website, you can make changes to improve the user experience.

3. **Increase customer loyalty:** By addressing customer concerns, you can improve customer loyalty. When customers feel that their feedback is valued and their concerns are addressed, they are more likely to continue doing business with your company.

4. **Gather valuable insights:** Exit surveys can provide valuable insights into customer preferences and behaviors. By analyzing the data collected through these surveys, you can gain a better understanding of your customer base and tailor your products and services accordingly.

To make the most of exit surveys, it is important to keep them short and focused. You should also make sure that the questions are clear and easy to understand. It is also important to analyze the data collected and act based on the insights gained from the surveys. By doing so, you can improve the customer experience, increase customer loyalty, and ultimately grow your business.

Exit surveys are just one of many methods to gather customer feedback. Another very important strategy is to request feedback through product and business reviews.

Customer feedback and reviews are essential for any eCommerce website looking to improve its products and services. By listening to your customers, you can identify areas for improvement and make changes that will ultimately lead to higher sales and greater customer satisfaction. Here's a detailed explanation of how to use customer feedback and reviews to improve your products and services:

1. **Collect customer feedback:** The first step is to actively collect customer feedback. You can do this through surveys, customer reviews, social media, and other channels. Encourage customers to share their thoughts and opinions on your products and services and make it easy for them to do so.

2. **Analyze feedback:** Once you have collected customer feedback, it's important to analyze it carefully. Look for patterns and trends in the feedback, and identify areas where customers are consistently expressing dissatisfaction or suggesting improvements.

3. **Take action:** Based on the feedback you receive, take action to make changes to your products and services. This could involve making changes to your product design, improving your customer service, or even changing your pricing strategy. Make sure to

communicate any changes you make to your customers and thank them for their feedback.

4. **Monitor progress:** It's important to monitor the impact of any changes you make. Keep track of customer feedback after you make changes and look for improvements in customer satisfaction and sales. If you don't see the results you were hoping for, be open to making further changes based on customer feedback.

5. **Encourage customer reviews:** Encouraging customers to leave reviews on your website and other platforms can be a powerful way to improve your products and services. Reviews can provide valuable insights into what customers like and don't like about your products and can help you identify areas for improvement.

6. **Respond to reviews:** When customers leave reviews, make sure to respond to them in a timely and professional manner. Address any concerns they raise and thank them for their feedback. This shows that you value their opinions and are committed to providing excellent customer service.

7. **Be open to criticism:** Don't get defensive when customers provide negative feedback. Instead, view it as an opportunity to improve your products and services.

8. **Use reviews in marketing:** Positive customer reviews can be a powerful marketing tool. Use them in your social media posts, email campaigns, and other marketing materials to showcase the quality of your products and services.

In conclusion, using customer feedback and reviews to improve your products and services is essential for any eCommerce website looking to succeed in today's competitive market. By actively collecting feedback, analyzing it, taking action, monitoring progress, encouraging customer reviews, responding to reviews, and using reviews in marketing, you can build a strong reputation for quality and customer satisfaction.

OPTIMIZE WITH A/B TESTING

A/B testing, also known as split testing, is a powerful technique used by eCommerce businesses to improve their website's performance and increase conversions. The process involves testing two versions of a web page or element against each other to see which one performs better. By conducting A/B tests, eCommerce businesses can determine which changes to their website design, content, or layout will have the greatest impact on customer behavior.

Here is a step-by-step guide to conducting effective A/B tests for eCommerce businesses:

1. **Define your goal:** The first step in conducting an A/B test is to define your goal. What do you want to achieve with this test? Do you want to increase sales, improve click-through rates, or boost engagement? Once you have identified your goal, you can then create a hypothesis about what changes you can make to achieve that goal.

2. **Identify the element to test:** The next step is to identify the element that you want to test. This could be a webpage headline, call-to-action button, or product image. Whatever element you choose to test, make sure it is significant enough to impact your goal and easy to measure.

3. **Create two versions:** With your goal and element to test identified, create two versions of the webpage or element. Version A should be your control, which is the original version, while Version B should be the variation that you want to test. Make sure that the two versions differ in one significant way, such as color, text, or layout.

4. **Choose your sample size:** The sample size is the number of people who will see your test. You need to ensure that your sample size is large enough to provide accurate results. Typically, a sample size of at least 100 visitors per variation is recommended.

5. **Run the test:** Once you have created the two versions and chosen your sample size, you can run the test. Use an A/B testing tool, such as Google Optimize or Optimizely, to randomly show Version A to one group of visitors and Version B to another. The tool will track the behavior of both groups and collect data on how they interact with each version.

6. **Analyze the results:** After running the test for a sufficient period, typically a few weeks, you can analyze the results. Look at the data collected by the testing tool to determine which version performed better in achieving your goal. If Version B performed better, it means that the change you made to that version had a positive impact on customer behavior.

7. **Implement the winning version:** If Version B performed better, implement the changes you made to that version on your website. If the changes you made had a positive impact on customer behavior, it is likely that they will continue to do so once implemented across your website.

8. **Rinse and repeat:** Once you have implemented the winning version, you can start the process again by identifying another element to test and repeating the A/B testing process. Over time, this will allow you to make incremental improvements to your website and increase your chances of achieving your goals.

There are numerous benefits of A/B testing for an eCommerce business, here are just a few.

1. **Improved Conversion Rates:** By conducting A/B tests, eCommerce businesses can identify the most effective version of their website in terms of conversion rates. This means that they can improve their website to attract and convert more visitors into customers.

2. **Increased Revenue:** Higher conversion rates mean more sales, which can lead to increased revenue for the eCommerce business. Even a small increase in conversion rates can have a significant impact on the bottom line.

3. **Better User Experience:** A/B testing can help eCommerce businesses to identify and fix issues with their website that may be impacting the user experience. This can include issues with page load times, confusing navigation, or unclear calls-to-action.

4. **Data-Driven Decision Making:** A/B testing provides valuable data that can be used to make informed decisions about website optimization. Instead of relying on assumptions or guesses about what will work best, eCommerce businesses can use real data to guide their decision-making process.

5. **Cost-Effective:** A/B testing is a relatively low-cost way to improve website performance compared to other marketing strategies. It allows eCommerce businesses to test and optimize their website without having to invest a significant amount of time or money.

6. **Competitive Advantage:** eCommerce businesses that use A/B testing to optimize their website are likely to have a competitive advantage over those that don't. By continuously improving their website, they can provide a better user experience and stay ahead of their competitors.

7. **Insights into Customer Behavior:** A/B testing can provide valuable insights into customer behavior, such as which products are most popular, which pages receive the most traffic, and which call-to-action buttons are most effective. This information can be used to inform future marketing and product development strategies.

In conclusion, A/B testing is a valuable tool for eCommerce businesses looking to improve their website performance and increase revenue. By conducting regular A/B tests, eCommerce businesses can optimize their website to provide a better user experience, increase conversion rates, and stay ahead of their competitors.

MONITOR YOUR WEBSITE
ANALYTICS REGULARLY

Data is King! Knowing more about how your website has been performing will allow you to make more informed decisions when it comes to improving your business.

Monitoring website analytics is a crucial step in ensuring the success of an eCommerce website. Analytics provide valuable insights into website performance, customer behavior, and conversion rates. By regularly tracking website analytics, eCommerce businesses can make data-driven decisions that can lead to increased sales and revenue.

There are several key metrics that eCommerce businesses should monitor to track website performance. These include:

1. **Traffic:** This refers to the number of visitors to the website over a specific period of time. Traffic can be broken down into new visitors and returning visitors.

2. **Conversion rate:** This is the percentage of website visitors who make a purchase. A high conversion rate indicates that the website is effective at turning visitors into customers.

3. **Average order value (AOV):** This refers to the average amount of money spent per order. Increasing the AOV can help boost revenue.

4. **Bounce rate:** This is the percentage of visitors who leave the website after viewing only one page. A high bounce rate can indicate that the website is not engaging or user-friendly.

5. **Time on site:** This refers to the amount of time visitors spend on the website. A longer time on site can indicate that visitors are engaged with the website and its content.

Once these metrics have been identified, eCommerce businesses can use website analytics tools to track them over time. Google Analytics is one of the most popular website analytics tools, and it is free to use. Other popular options include Adobe Analytics and Piwik PRO.

To make the most of website analytics, eCommerce businesses should establish goals and key performance indicators (KPIs) for their website. These goals and KPIs should be specific, measurable, and aligned with the overall business objectives. For example, an eCommerce business might set a goal of increasing the conversion rate by 5% over the next quarter.

Once goals and KPIs have been established, eCommerce businesses can use website analytics to measure progress towards these goals. They can also use analytics to identify areas for improvement and make data-driven decisions about website design, content, and marketing.

One way to use website analytics to improve website performance is to conduct A/B testing. A/B testing involves creating two versions of a web page and testing them against each other to see which one performs better. For example, an eCommerce business might create two versions of a product page with different product descriptions and images. They can then use website analytics to track the performance of each page and identify the version that results in more sales.

Another way to use website analytics to improve website performance is to track customer behavior on the website. This can include tracking the pages they visit, the products they view, and the items they add to their cart. By analyzing this data, eCommerce businesses can identify patterns and make data-driven decisions about website design and product offerings.

Customer feedback and reviews can also be valuable sources of information for eCommerce businesses. By monitoring customer feedback and reviews, eCommerce businesses can identify areas for improvement and make changes to improve the customer experience. They can also use customer feedback to identify popular products and make data-driven decisions about product offerings.

To encourage customers to leave feedback and reviews, eCommerce businesses can use email marketing campaigns and social media. They can also offer incentives, such as a discount on their next purchase, for customers who leave a review.

In conclusion, monitoring website analytics is an essential part of running a successful eCommerce business. By tracking metrics such as traffic, conversion rate, and average order value, eCommerce businesses can make data-driven decisions about website design, content, and marketing. They can also use website analytics to conduct A/B testing, track customer behavior, and identify areas for improvement. By using customer feedback and reviews, eCommerce businesses can make changes to improve the customer experience and increase sales and revenue.

ATTEND TRADE SHOWS AND EVENTS

Attending trade shows and events is an effective way for eCommerce brands to network and showcase their products. Here are some reasons why eCommerce brands should consider attending trade shows and events:

1. **Networking Opportunities:** Trade shows and events provide eCommerce brands with an opportunity to meet other professionals and business owners in their industry. This can lead to potential partnerships, collaborations, and even new customers.

2. **Brand Exposure:** Attending trade shows and events can increase brand exposure and visibility. eCommerce brands can showcase their products and services to a wider audience, potentially leading to increased sales and customer acquisition.

3. **Market Research:** Trade shows and events allow eCommerce brands to gather market research and insights. They can observe the

trends and behaviors of their target audience, learn about new industry developments, and gain valuable knowledge about their competitors.

4. **Face-to-Face Interaction:** Trade shows and events provide an opportunity for eCommerce brands to interact with their customers face-to-face. This can create a more personal connection and build trust with customers, potentially leading to increased loyalty and customer retention.

5. **Learning Opportunities:** Trade shows and events often offer educational seminars and workshops for attendees. eCommerce brands can learn about new marketing strategies, industry developments, and best practices from experts in their field.

Overall, attending trade shows and events can provide numerous benefits for eCommerce brands. They can increase brand exposure, provide networking opportunities, gather market research, create personal connections with customers, and offer learning opportunities.

CONCLUSION

We have covered a lot of information in this book and now you have all the building blocks required to develop a successful eCommerce business. The key takeaways you need from this book are that Data is King. It is crucial to understand your product, your target audience, your website, and everything about your business. The only way to improve is to know what needs to be improved. Focus on providing an excellent product, even better customer service, and always be in search of that perfect email subject line, or ad copy.

Times and trends are always changing, so it's important to stay up to date with what's new, what new strategies there are and how you can best engage with your customers.

Technology is always being improved as well, so don't settle with your platform, software or any other tech just because it works. Review your stack every year and improve wherever possible. Is there a better website solution, are there any new payment options available? You need to stay on top of it all the time.

Keep a close eye on your competitors, the big players who have huge marketing and technology budgets are always good to watch. If you see competitors using new techniques, designs or concepts, you should see if you can adapt as well.

Don't let this be the end of your learning journey, there is still a lot to learn. I could write individual books for each section in this book, and perhaps I will. But in the meantime, don't forget to subscribe to my newsletter so I can send you more detailed information and mini eBooks on the subjects mentioned in this book, plus much more.

Visit **www.savvyweb.net/newsletter**

www.ingramcontent.com/pod-product-compliance
Lightning Source LLC
Chambersburg PA
CBHW070340220526
45467CB00001B/194